WORLD MYTHS AND LEGENDS

Greek & Roman

Joanne Suter

Fearon/Janus
Belmont, CA

Simon & Schuster Supplementary Education Group

World Myths and Legends

Greek and Roman
Ancient Middle Eastern
Norse
African
Far Eastern
Celtic
Native American
Regional American

Series Editor: Joseph T. Curran
Cover Designer: Dianne Platner
Text Designer: Teresa A. Holden
Interior Illustrations: James McConnell
Cover Photo: Lowie Museum of Anthropology,
    The University of California at Berkeley

Library of Congress Catalog Card Number: 91-72586

ISBN 0-8224-4636-7

Printed in the United States of America

1. 9 8 7 6 5 4 3 2 1

CONTENTS

An Introduction to Greek and Roman Mythology

Our desire to understand the world we live in is as old as history. Why does the sun travel across the sky? Why do the stars come out at night? How did the world begin? Why is there suffering? Today we take many of our answers from science. But we're still searching.

Long ago, such things were described in stories of gods, goddesses, and heroes. We call these stories *myths*. Myths are different from *legends* and *folk tales*. All three entertain and instruct. But myths go deeper. They point to the power and mystery we sense in our lives. They wake us up to these qualities.

The gods and goddesses of ancient Greece and Rome lived on a high mountain called Mount Olympus. But they were very much like human beings. They were grand and mighty, yes, but they also made mistakes. They laughed and loved and got angry.

Poets and musicians put the myths together. Travelers spread them throughout the ancient lands. The myths were passed down over thousands of years, and they're still studied today. Movies, plays, and novels repeat their themes. Greek and Roman myths offer as much romance and adventure as the latest Hollywood release. They help us understand the people of the past who told them, and they help us understand ourselves.

The Major Gods and Goddesses of Greece and Rome

Greek and Roman myths tell of similar gods and goddesses. This table lists the most important ones.

Description	Greek Name	Roman Name
king of the gods; lord of the sky	Zeus	Jupiter
queen of the gods; protector of married women	Hera	Juno
god of the sea; brother of Zeus; gave humankind the horse	Poseidon	Neptune
god of the underworld; brother of Zeus	Hades	Pluto
goddess of grain	Demeter	Ceres

Description	Greek Name	Roman Name
goddess of love and beauty; born from the sea on a bed of foam	Aphrodite	Venus
god of the sun; god of music and song; taught mortals the art of healing	Apollo	Apollo
god of war	Ares	Mars
goddess of the moon; the huntress	Artemis	Diana
goddess of wisdom; goddess of the city	Athena	Minerva
god of wine	Dionysus	Bacchus
god of metalworkers and craftsmen; forged the armor of the gods; Aphrodite's husband	Hephaestus	Vulcan
Zeus's messenger; god of thieves; wore winged hat and sandals	Hermes	Mercury

Out of the Darkness

The Greeks of long ago had their own ideas about how the world came to be.

In the beginning there was nothing. There was only empty space. Then, out of the darkness, Mother Earth appeared. Mother Earth brought wonderful things to fill the darkness. She brought beauty and light and day.

Father Sky also came out of that darkness. Father Sky spread out above the earth and covered her with stars.

Mother Earth and Father Sky brought forth children. Some of their children were called the Titans. They were huge and strong. They held the strength of the volcano, of the earthquake, of the storm.

Some of Mother Earth's and Father Sky's children were called the Cyclopes. Each Cyclops had a single eye in the middle of his forehead. The giant eye was as large as a wheel.

And some of the children were frightening creatures, each with 50 heads and 100 arms. Father Sky was afraid of these children.

Their powerful arms could stir up the sea. They could shake the world! Father Sky could not bear to look at their terrible waving arms. So he hid those children deep beneath the ground. He put them in the darkness, where light could not get in and they could not get out.

Mother Earth was very sad. She loved her children of the hundred arms. They might be ugly monsters, but they were still her children! She was angry that Father Sky had hidden them away.

Mother Earth called the Titans together. "My tall, strong children," she said, "your father must be punished. He has treated your brothers of the hundred arms most cruelly. You must help me to get even with him!"

The Titans were afraid. Only one was brave enough to stand up against his father. Cronus was the youngest of the Titans. "I will do as you ask, Mother," he said. "Tell me what I must do."

Mother Earth gave her giant son a metal sickle. It was strong and gray and had jagged teeth along the edge. "Arm yourself with this," she cried. "And lie in wait for your father."

Mighty Cronus wounded his father with that sickle. Father Sky's blood ran into the seas. With this terrible wound, he could no longer be a ruler. Then the Titan Cronus, with his wife, Rhea, set out to rule the universe.

1. *How is a Cyclops different from a Titan?*
2. *Why did Mother Earth want to punish Father Sky?*
3. *Who was the bravest of the Titans?*

Zeus Becomes King of the Gods

This Greek myth explains how the earth came to be ruled by the gods on Mount Olympus.

The great Titan Cronus ruled the universe with his wife, Rhea. But he was not happy. He remembered how he had hurt his father. And he worried that his own children would turn against him.

"We'll see about that!" Cronus roared. He began to swallow his children, one after another, as soon as they were born.

"No!" cried Rhea. For, like Mother Earth, she loved her children. But she could not stop Cronus from gulping down the babies.

At last she went to Mother Earth for help. When the next child, Zeus, was born, Mother Earth stole the baby boy away. She hid him in a deep cave on a mountainside. Then Rhea wrapped a giant stone in blankets. She pretended this well-wrapped stone was the baby Zeus. She watched as Cronus grabbed the stone and swallowed it down.

Mother Earth watched over Zeus as he grew. When he was strong and ready, Zeus went to Cronus with some magic wine. The

4

wine made his father very sick. Cronus threw up the five children he had swallowed in the past. They were still alive. The stone that Cronus had been told was Zeus also came up. That very stone remains today just where it fell. It is in a place called Delphi.

Then there was a terrible war. For ten years, Zeus and his five brothers and sisters fought against Cronus and the other Titans. Their battles almost wrecked the universe!

At first it seemed the Titans would win. But Zeus asked the one-eyed Cyclopes to help him. They made thunderbolts for Zeus to use as weapons. Then Zeus set free the hundred-armed giants from beneath the ground. They threw great rocks at the Titans. The earth shook. The sky rumbled. Zeus threw his thunderbolts. Lightning flashed. The forests caught fire, and the sea boiled, but at last the Titans were beaten. The hundred-armed giants took them deep beneath the ground to the underworld.

A few of the Titans escaped the underworld. One, a giant named Atlas, had been given a different punishment. Zeus gave him the job of holding the whole world on his mighty shoulders. From that day on, Atlas would stand in a place wrapped in clouds and darkness.

Atlas held up the world

Zeus became king of the gods. He and two of his brothers drew lots to decide what each of them should rule. Zeus, with his thunderbolts and lightning, became ruler of the heavens. Poseidon became god of the sea. Hades ruled the underworld.

Then there was peace. Zeus had great palaces built on top of Mount Olympus. There the gods lived and slept. They drank sweet drinks and listened to beautiful music. No clouds or rain or snow ever bothered them. They lived forever in sunshine.

1. *Why did Cronus swallow his children?*

2. *Which child was hidden from Cronus?*

3. *What weapon did the Cyclopes make for Zeus?*

The Creation of Man and the Gift of Fire

The Greeks say the task of creating man was given to a Titan named Prometheus. Because of Prometheus's kindness, people were able to live comfortably on the earth.

Zeus, the great ruler, decided that it was time for animals and people to appear on earth. He gave the job of making the creatures to two Titan brothers, Prometheus and Epimetheus.

Prometheus was very wise. He had helped Zeus fight in the war against the other Titans. His name means *forethought*. Prometheus always thought things over carefully before deciding what to do.

Prometheus had a brother named Epimetheus. His name means *afterthought*. Epimetheus always acted without thinking.

In the great war between Zeus and the Titans, Epimetheus had not taken sides. He had helped no one, and had hurt no one.

Prometheus and Epimetheus were to make all the men and all the animals. Epimetheus, without a thought, set right to work on the animals. He hurried about, giving the animals all the best gifts. He gave them speed and strength. He gave the birds wings so they could fly. He gave the animals a sharp sense of smell, fierce claws, and warm fur. When Epimetheus was ready to make men, he had given the best gifts away. He could think of nothing more.

"Look what you have done, brother!" Prometheus cried. "Once again, you acted too quickly. You didn't think."

"What can I do now?" Epimetheus worried. He could see that the people were going to be in big trouble. "Brother, can you help me?"

"Of course," Prometheus answered. He set to work, thinking hard as he began to create man. Prometheus mixed earth and water together. He decided to mold man in a shape different from the other animals. He used the shape of the gods themselves. He let man walk upright on two legs instead of four.

Prometheus watched the new creatures walk about on the earth. He saw them shiver in the cold. He saw that they were still weaker than the animals. He figured out a way to help.

Prometheus went to the blacksmith shop

of the god Hephaestus. There he found a great fire burning. Hephaestus used the fire to forge the shields and weapons of the gods. Prometheus stole a tiny spark from the fire. He hid the spark between his hands and carried it back to earth. This would be his gift to man.

Zeus was angry! Prometheus had stolen the fire of the gods and given it away. Zeus was also worried. Perhaps the gift of fire would make man too strong. Fire was not meant for human hands!

"Prometheus must pay for this!" Zeus thundered. Zeus's eyes flashed. His terrible temper shook the earth.

Since Prometheus was a Titan, he could not be killed. But Zeus had something worse than death in mind. He ordered Prometheus to a faraway mountain where he was chained to a rock.

"You have dared to steal from the gods!" Zeus roared. "You shall feel pain forever!"

Zeus sent a huge eagle to the rock where Prometheus lay chained. Every day the eagle came and pecked at Prometheus's liver, and every night his liver grew back. Prometheus lay chained to the rock for years and years. But wise Prometheus waited patiently. He knew one day a great hero would come and set him free. That, however, is another tale.

1. *What do the names "Prometheus" and "Epimetheus" mean?*

2. *Why was Zeus angry at Prometheus for giving fire to people?*

3. *How was Prometheus punished for giving away fire?*

Pandora's Box

Where do trouble, pain, and sorrow come from? In this myth, the ancient Greeks tell how these things appeared on earth.

Zeus was angry at the men who walked the earth. They had accepted the gift of fire! He decided their punishment would be brought to earth by the first woman. This was Pandora.

All the gods and goddesses gave Pandora gifts before she was sent to earth. Aphrodite gave her beauty and charm. Apollo gave her the gift of music. Athena gave her wisdom. And someone, some say it was Zeus himself, gave her the gift of curiosity. Then Zeus handed Pandora a lovely golden box. It had a very tight lid. Zeus told Pandora to take the box with her to earth. "But," he warned her, "you must never, never open it."

Zeus sent Pandora to Epimetheus. "She is your gift for making all those animals for the earth," Zeus said.

Prometheus had warned Epimetheus never to accept gifts from Zeus. But Epimetheus saw how lovely Pandora was.

He forgot his brother's words. Epimetheus fell in love with Pandora. They became husband and wife.

Pandora put her box on a high shelf. She remembered Zeus's warning. She told herself she'd never open the golden box. But in time her curiosity grew stronger and stronger. One day, when Epimetheus was away, she climbed up to the shelf.

"I must know what is inside this box!" Pandora said. "Just one little peek couldn't hurt. Since it comes from the gods, it must be something wonderful!"

Pandora shook the box a little. She heard something scurry about inside it. This made her all the more curious. She lifted the lid just the slightest crack.

Suddenly the box seemed to leap out of her hands. The lid fell off, and the most terrible things came flying out of it. Roars, screams, howls, and moans filled the room. It grew very dark. Awful things came out of that box. Some had wings. Some slithered and crawled. Some had pointed ears, long tails, and sharp fangs. These creatures were envy, greed, sickness, and sorrow. They were hunger and prejudice, and evil of every kind.

"Oh, no!" Pandora cried. She knew she had done something terribly wrong. She

Pandora's curiosity

slammed the lid down on the box. But it was too late. The creatures had escaped. They swirled away, carried by the wind to every corner of the earth. Only one, called Hope, remained inside. Hope stayed in order to help humans fight what had escaped Pandora's box.

1. *Who gave Pandora the box?*
2. *What flew out of Pandora's box?*
3. *What warning did Prometheus give Epimetheus?*

Demeter and Persephone: A Story of the Seasons

This myth tells about beautiful Persephone and her mother, the harvest goddess Demeter. It also explains the changing of the seasons.

Persephone was the lovely daughter of Demeter, goddess of all that grows on earth. Persephone was very, very beautiful, and her mother loved her dearly.

One fine morning Persephone was picking wildflowers along a stream. All of a sudden a dark figure appeared. His shadow blocked the sunlight. It was Hades, god of the underworld, king of the dead.

Hades had been watching Persephone. He admired her beauty. In fact, the lonely lord of darkness had fallen in love with her.

Hades was powerful. He was used to getting what he wanted. He grabbed Persephone and carried her to his chariot. Four black horses pulled the chariot away.

"Mother! Mother!" the frightened girl cried as she was carried off.

Demeter heard her daughter's call. She hurried to find her, but Persephone was gone. A dark hole had opened in the ground. Hades had carried her down to the underworld, the land of the dead.

Demeter's heart was broken. She decided to search the world until she had found her daughter.

Demeter dressed herself as an old woman in a black cloak. She wandered the earth looking for Persephone. Wherever she went, she asked people if they had seen her daughter. But anyone who had a clue for Demeter was afraid to help. No one wanted to anger Hades.

Demeter was very sad. She forgot her duties as goddess of growing things. All green things on earth withered and died. No crops grew in the fields. The leaves fell from the trees. The earth was cold and empty.

Zeus, king of the gods, saw the bare earth. He saw people starving because no food grew.

"This must stop!" Zeus told Demeter.

But Demeter was angry. "I will not allow one seed to grow," she said, "until I have my daughter back again!"

Zeus knew that something had to be done. If not, all the people on earth would die of hunger. Hades was powerful, and he was Zeus's brother. But Zeus's power was greatest of all. Whatever Zeus commanded would be done.

Zeus sent his messenger, Hermes, to the underworld. "Send Persephone back to her mother," Zeus commanded.

Hades knew he had to obey. But he'd grown to love Persephone deeply in the months she'd been with him. Hades had given Persephone beautiful clothing and a crown of dark jewels. The pale unhappy queen sat on the throne beside him.

Persephone was so sad she had refused to eat. During her stay in the underworld, she had eaten only four pomegranate seeds.

"You must let Persephone return home," Hermes said. "It is Zeus's order."

But Hades knew he could keep his lovely queen. "She has eaten the seeds of the pomegranate," he said. "No one may leave once they have eaten the food of the dead!"

Persephone cried. She begged Hades to let her go. "Just let me visit my mother," she sobbed. "I promise I will return to you."

So Hades allowed Persephone to leave. He let Hermes take her back to Demeter. But he made Persephone swear to return.

"You ate four pomegranate seeds," Hades said. "You will return and stay with me four months of every year." Then he turned away, for he could not bear to watch her go. Persephone rode home in the golden chariot drawn by the black horses.

Demeter met Persephone in an empty field. As soon as she saw her daughter, she threw off her black cloak. She stood tall and golden in the sunlight. At that instant, blades of grass sprang up in the field. Leaves and blossoms appeared on the trees. The earth was green and fruitful again.

And so it was. Each year, as she had promised, Persephone went to live with Hades. For four long months of every year, the earth felt Demeter's sorrow. It became bare and cold, and nothing grew. This was winter. And each time Persephone returned to Demeter, the earth rejoiced. It brought forth flowers, fruit, and growing things. And this was spring.

1. *Where did Hades take Persephone, and why did he take her?*

2. *What did Persephone eat while she was in the underworld?*

3. *What happened to the earth while Demeter was off looking for Persephone?*

Daedalus and Icarus:
A Story of Flight

Have you ever wanted to fly? The Greeks told of a young man who could. But Icarus tried to fly where his wings could not take him.

On the island of Crete lived a great inventor. Daedalus could build anything! The ruler of the island, King Minos, kept Daedalus very busy. Daedalus designed palaces and made statues for the king.

Now King Minos had a terrible beast called a Minotaur. The king needed a safe place to keep the monster. So he had Daedalus design a complicated maze with winding passages. There King Minos kept the Minotaur trapped.

King Minos wanted to keep Daedalus trapped, too. He did not want him making things for other kingdoms. He wanted to keep Daedalus's talents all to himself. The king ordered Daedalus and his son, Icarus, to stay on Crete. He said that no ships could carry them off the island.

But Daedalus was smart. He knew there had to be a way to escape. Watching gulls soar over the ocean, he had an idea. "King Minos cannot trap the birds on his island. And he shall not trap me or my son!"

Daedalus set right to work. He and Icarus collected feathers they found on the shore. They also trapped gulls and pulled off their feathers. They carefully stored the feathers in a cave by the sea.

Daedalus studied the way the birds took off. He watched how they flew. He studied the bones in their wings. Then he began to build wings. He made frames with thin pieces of wood. He attached feathers to the frames with thread and wax. At last Daedalus had a pair of wings larger than those of the largest bird. Then he made a smaller pair for Icarus.

When all was ready, Daedalus strapped the wings to his arms. He strapped the smaller wings to Icarus. "Be still, son, and listen carefully," Daedalus said.

Icarus was excited, but he listened to his father's words.

"Stay near me as we fly away," Daedalus told Icarus. "Watch me, and do only as I do. Remember not to fly too close to the sea. If you do, your wings might get wet and heavy. They will drag you down. But do not fly too high, either. The sun could melt the wax that holds your feathers together!"

Then Daedalus ran to the edge of the cliff. "Follow me!" he cried. As the wind caught his wings, he rose into the air.

Icarus followed. He ran and flapped his arms as his father had done. And he felt the wind lift him. He rose higher and higher.

At first Icarus stayed close behind his father. They moved steadily across the sky. But the young boy soon began playing. He dipped and glided and made loops in the air.

"Father is too old to enjoy this!" he cried. Young Icarus flew toward the heavens. People below looked up in amazement. They could not believe what they were seeing.

"Icarus, come back!" Daedalus shouted. But the wind snatched away his words. Icarus could not hear him. Daedalus watched the boy fly higher and higher into the sun. Soon he was only a speck in Daedalus's eye.

Daedalus tried to follow Icarus, to catch him, to call him back. But it was too late. The sun had done its work. The wax that held the feathers had melted. Icarus's wings were falling apart! Daedalus saw his son falling to earth. There was nothing he could do to save his boy. Icarus flapped his arms wildly. Then he fell into the sea.

Daedalus circled round and round for hours. But the white ocean foam had closed

Icarus flew higher and higher

over Icarus. There was nothing to see. At last Daedalus flew on. When he reached land, he was sobbing. Daedalus took off his wings and hid them away forever. It is wrong, he decided. It is wrong for people to soar like the birds or the gods.

1. *Why did King Minos want Daedalus and his son to stay on Crete?*

2. *What gave Daedalus his idea for getting off the island?*

3. *Why didn't Icarus listen to his father's warning?*

Midas

Sometimes wealth seems like the most important thing in the world. And sometimes our own ideas seem much more important than anyone else's. Here are two stories about a man whose beliefs caused him some trouble.

The Golden Apples

In the kingdom of Phrygia lived a king named Midas. He was powerful and rich, and he loved gold more than anything in the world.

In most ways, Midas was a good king. He had a kind heart and was fair to his people. One day an old man appeared at the palace door. He said he had lost his way and was very tired. Midas ordered that the man be given food and drink and a place to sleep for the night. In the morning, the traveler was on his way. Midas did not think any more about the visit.

But a few days later, another visitor came before the King. Midas recognized him. It was none other than Dionysus, the god of wine. Midas could hardly believe his eyes.

"Midas," said the great god, "you have shown kindness to a stranger. The man you helped was a dear friend of mine. The gods reward such kindness. You may have one wish. What would you like most of all?"

"What luck!" King Midas thought. He lost no time in answering the god. "Gold!" he cried. "I wish everything I touch would turn to gold!"

Dionysus shook his head. "You have made a poor choice," he said sadly. "But I promised you a wish, and so it shall be."

King Midas was excited. As soon as Dionysus disappeared, he hurried to try out his new gift. He rushed into the garden, reached up, and picked an apple from a tree.

"Ha!" Midas laughed aloud. In his hand he held a golden apple.

King Midas ran through his garden touching everything in sight. "Oh, joy!" he cried. Everything he touched turned to gold!

Midas went back inside the palace. Soon he had golden chairs and golden tables. He had windowsills and doorknobs and shutters all made of solid gold. At last he felt tired from all the excitement. He was hungry, too.

"Bring me my supper!" the king called to his servants. He sat down at the golden table. A fine dinner was served. Midas raised a bit of food to his lips and tried to take a bite.

"Ouch!" he howled as he bit down on something hard as stone. He spit the thing into his hand. Midas saw that what had once been food was now a piece of gold. Then he raised a wine glass to his lips. Chunks of gold poured out of it.

Midas became very frightened. "I will starve to death! I'll die of hunger!"

Dionysus had been right. Midas had made a poor choice indeed.

But King Midas was a lucky mortal. And Dionysus was a kind god. Once more Dionysus appeared before Midas.

"Have you learned your lesson?" Dionysus asked. "Then go to the Pactolus River and swim in its waters. You will be freed of the golden touch."

King Midas listened to the god and hurried to the river. He jumped in. When he came out, he found he had lost the golden touch. The gold had passed from his body into the river. From that day forth, the sands of the Pactolus River sparkled with gold.

1. *Which god gave Midas the "Midas touch," and why?*

2. *Why did Dionysus say that Midas had made a poor choice?*

3. *How did Dionysus reverse the spell for Midas?*

The Music Contest

King Midas had learned a very valuable lesson. Never again would he want riches and treasures. In fact, he even lost interest in his fine palace. Now the king loved to wander in the forests, to walk through the meadows, to feel the soft breezes. He worshiped Pan, the god of the forests and fields.

Pan was a god who took an unusual form. He was half man and half goat. Pan spent his days playing music on pipes made from river reeds.

"Your music is the most beautiful in the world!" King Midas told Pan. "It is more beautiful than the tunes Apollo plays upon his lyre."

Apollo himself heard King Midas's words. "We must have a contest," the god said. "I will play my lyre, and you, Pan, will play your pipes. We shall see whose music is the most beautiful."

Apollo asked Tmolus, the mountain, to judge the contest.

First Pan played. The high sweet music of his pipes floated on the breeze. The trees swayed to it.

Then Apollo played. The notes from his silver lyre filled the air. The music was strong and pure. The woodland animals stopped to listen. As he played, Apollo sang softly. He sang of heroes, of love, and of the gods on Mount Olympus. Pan put down his pipes to listen. Tmolus declared Apollo the winner.

But King Midas disagreed. He cried out that Pan was still the best musician.

Apollo grew angry. "You do not know what you hear!" he shouted at Midas. "You have ears like an ass!"

At that moment, King Midas had a strange feeling in his head. Suddenly, his ears began to grow. They became larger and larger. Midas looked at his reflection in a stream. His ears were now long and furry. Apollo had given him the ears of an ass!

King Midas begged and pleaded. But Apollo would not return his human ears.

King Midas wrapped a red turban tightly about his head. He would let no one in the kingdom see his ears! But the time came when Midas needed a haircut. So he called in the royal barber.

"You must never tell anyone what you are about to see!" King Midas ordered. Then he unwound the turban.

The barber cut the king's hair and went on his way. He knew he would have to keep the secret of the king's ears. If he didn't he would be put to death.

But the barber liked to talk. He wanted to tell the secret just to say the words. His wife began to complain that he was talking in his sleep. The barber knew that one day he would let the secret out.

So the barber went far into a meadow. He dug a hole in the ground near a stream. He bent down and put his mouth against the hole. "King Midas has ass's ears," he whispered into the hole. Then he covered over the hole with dirt and leaves. "There!" he said. "I feel much better now."

Nothing happened for a time. Then one day some people were passing through the meadow. "Listen!" they said.

Reeds had grown up from that hole the barber had dug. The wind rustled the reeds as it blew through them. The tall reeds whispered, "King Midas has ass's ears . . . ass's ears . . . ass's ears."

4. *Who was Midas's favorite musician? What instrument did he play?*

5. *What god was angered by Midas's choice?*

6. *What kind of animal's ears did Apollo give Midas?*

Echo and Narcissus

This myth tells about a young man who thought too highly of himself.

Deep in the forests lived fairy-like creatures called nymphs. They made their homes in the streams and in the trees and flowers.

One of these lovely beings was named Echo. She was sweet and beautiful. But she had one fault. Echo talked too much. She always made sure she had the last word in any conversation or argument. Hera, queen of the gods, heard the nymph's constant talking. After a time, it made her angry. She decided to put a stop to Echo's chatter.

"From this day," Hera said, "you shall not be able to speak your own words. I know you are fond of having the last say. But the last words will no longer be yours. You will only repeat the last words that other people say."

So Echo wandered the forest, calling back to people their last words. One day she saw a young man named Narcissus. He was hunting alone in the woods. Narcissus was very handsome. Echo fell in love with him at once. She longed to speak, but she could not.

Narcissus heard a sound. "Who's here?" he called out.

"Here, here," was all Echo could say.

"Come!" Narcissus called.

"Come!" repeated Echo.

"Where are you?" asked Narcissus.

"You, you." Echo could stand it no longer. She rushed from her hiding place and threw her arms around Narcissus.

Narcissus knew what a handsome man he was. Many young women had fallen in love with him. He was quite proud of himself. And he was quite sure no one was good enough for him. He pulled back from Echo. "Really!" he frowned. "Who do you think you are? You certainly shall not have me!"

Echo's heart was broken. From then on, she hid in canyons and caves. She grew pale and thin. Finally her body wasted away. All that was left was her voice. Forever she would answer those who called out in her hiding places.

Narcissus went on, still thinking he was too handsome and fine for anyone. At last one young woman called out to the gods in anger. "Oh, goddess of love, make this proud man suffer. Make him know what it's like to love someone who doesn't return the love."

The young woman's prayer was heard.

Narcissus in love

There was a clear pond in the middle of the forest. Narcissus bent to drink from it. In the water, he saw his own reflection.

"Who is this beautiful creature?" Narcissus cried. He had fallen in love with himself!

Narcissus reached out to touch the beautiful being in the water. But when he touched the water, the creature disappeared. He drew back. When the water calmed, the being reappeared. Narcissus again tried to touch the face in the water. And again it disappeared.

"Why do you leave me?" Narcissus cried. "I am not ugly. Many have loved me. Even you look at me with love. When I reach out to you, you do the same."

Narcissus's tears fell into the pond. They rippled the water. The being disappeared.

"Stay!" Narcissus cried. "If I can't touch you, I will just look at you."

Narcissus would not leave the pool. Now he knew how it felt to love without having the love returned. He would not leave the pond to eat. He would not leave to sleep. Narcissus grew weaker and weaker.

Echo came near him. She could not be seen. But she called back to him when he spoke.

"Alas, alas," Narcissus sighed.

"Alas, alas," called Echo.

Finally Narcissus died. His spirit crossed the river that circles the land of the dead. As it did so, it leaned over the edge of the boat. It wanted to have one last look at the face in the water.

The nymphs came to bury Narcissus's body. But he was nowhere to be found. A single beautiful flower bloomed in the place he had knelt. The nymphs called it the narcissus.

1. *What are nymphs, and where were they said to live?*

2. *Who stopped Echo's constant talking?*

3. *What grew where Narcissus died?*

Arachne

In Greek myths, the gods did not smile on mortals who had too much pride.

A young woman named Arachne lived with her father in a tiny village. Her father was a wool dyer. He colored wool all the shades of the rainbow. Arachne had learned to spin the wool into thread and to weave beautiful cloth. She became quite well known for her work. People came from near and far to see Arachne's weavings.

"The cloth is so soft!" they'd exclaim.

"And see how swiftly her hands move."

"You are so talented," one woman said. "Surely the great goddess Athena taught you herself!"

Arachne was very proud of her skill. It angered her to think that the goddess and not herself would get the credit.

"Why, I gained this skill myself!" Arachne answered the woman. "I practiced day and night. I need no help from a goddess! As for Athena, how could her cloth be finer than mine? Look at my work! Surely even she could not do such a job."

Athena was displeased when she heard Arachne's boasts. One day, Arachne found an old woman standing at her door with the other onlookers. The woman was dressed in a shabby black cloak. She leaned on a stick as she peered in at Arachne.

"Foolish girl," the woman said. "I am old and wise. And I know it is a mistake to claim to be equal to the gods. You should ask pardon from Athena for your words. Be happy as the best among mortals. But don't be so proud as to challenge the gods!"

"Stupid old woman!" Arachne cried. "I am not afraid. I meant what I said. I challenge Athena to a contest. Let her come forward, if she dare. Let her try her skill against mine."

"She comes!" the old woman answered, as she threw off her cloak. Before Arachne's eyes, the woman grew tall and strong.

The people in the doorway fell back a step. Arachne turned pale. But Arachne was very proud and would not give in. She gathered her courage and spoke to the goddess.

"Then let us begin the contest," she said.

Arachne went to one of her two large looms. Athena went to the other. Athena wove quickly. Her shuttle seemed to fly. The crowd was silent as pictures grew out of the cloth. The scenes Athena wove showed the gods in all their power. There was Poseidon, ruling over the mighty seas. There was Ares, dressed for battle.

Athena finished her work first. She stepped back and looked at Arachne's loom.

Arachne was angry that Athena had tricked her with a disguise. She was weaving pictures that showed the gods' weaknesses. Arachne showed the gods playing tricks on mortals. She showed them arguing among themselves.

Athena glared at Arachne's work. She grabbed the shuttle from Arachne's hand and threw it to the floor. Then she struck Arachne across the face.

Arachne was full of shame. "I cannot live with this insult!" she cried. Then she rushed out into the woods and hanged herself.

Athena felt sorry for Arachne. She touched Arachne's body and said, "Live, wicked girl. You shall continue to spin and weave. And so shall those who come after you."

As Athena spoke, Arachne's body became smaller and smaller. Her arms and legs grew thin. Arachne was changed into a tiny, brown spider hanging from a thread.

"Mortals will look at you," Athena said. "And remember that it isn't wise to match themselves against the gods."

Arachne's children still can be seen hanging from the threads they weave into webs.

1. *What scenes did Arachne put into her weavings? What scenes did Athena weave into hers?*

2. *How was Athena disguised when she appeared before Arachne?*

3. *How did Athena punish Arachne?*

Pygmalion

Sometimes the goddess of love and beauty hears a mortal's prayers. Pygmalion is a love story with a happy ending.

Pygmalion was a sculptor. He carved statues from ivory, marble, and other stones. Pygmalion was young and handsome. Many young women tried to catch his eye. But Pygmalion seldom looked at the young ladies. He kept busy with his work. Pygmalion had never been very interested in romance. Besides, he thought his statues were more attractive than real people.

One day Pygmalion began work on an ivory statue. As time passed, he realized that this figure was the most beautiful he had ever carved. It was of a slim, lovely woman. As he worked on the statue, it became more and more wonderful. At last he finished it. This time, Pygmalion thought, I have made something that is perfect.

Now Pygmalion could think of nothing but his ivory statue. He could not bring himself to begin another work. At night he dreamed the maiden came alive. She touched his hand

and kissed his lips. Pygmalion dreamed that her name was Galatea.

Night after night, Pygmalion had the same dream. Day after day he sat staring at his statue. Pygmalion thought her far more beautiful than any woman in the world. Sometimes he thought he saw her move! Then he would touch her. But the statue remained cold and hard.

For a while, Pygmalion pretended Galatea was alive. He brought her presents he thought a young woman might like. He brought little birds, bright flowers, and colored beads. He even dressed the statue and hung earrings on. And in the end he gave up. He knew he loved a lifeless form. He knew she would never love him back.

Pygmalion had always honored Aphrodite, the goddess of beauty. When the day came for Aphrodite's festival, Pygmalion went to her temple. The air there was filled with the smell of perfume. People approached the altar and asked Aphrodite to bless their romances. Pygmalion didn't dare ask for the gift he really wanted. Instead he asked, "Aphrodite, grant me a wife who is like my statue."

Aphrodite heard Pygmalion. She knew what his real wish was. And she was pleased that his work had brought the world so much beauty. The fire that burned low on the altar leaped into a bright flame. Pygmalion knew it was a sign. He hurried home. He was very excited. But he didn't know what to expect.

Galatea was as white and still as Pygmalion had left her. Pygmalion looked lovingly at the statue. As he did so, she seemed to move.

"It's only my imagination," Pygmalion thought. "My mind has played these tricks before." But his heart beat faster. And he went to Galatea and put his arms around her.

And then Pygmalion felt the hard cold ivory become like wax softening in the sun. He felt the blood begin to throb and flow beneath Galatea's skin!

"Thank you, sweet Aphrodite," Pygmalion whispered. He pressed his lips against Galatea's. Her lips had grown warm and soft. And as Pygmalion watched Galatea's face, her cheeks blushed pink. Galatea looked into Pygmalion's eyes. Pygmalion saw his love returned.

Aphrodite herself was a guest at the wedding of Galatea and Pygmalion.

1. *Why did Aphrodite want to help Pygmalion?*

2. *What sign told Pygmalion that Aphrodite would help him?*

3. *Why did Pygmalion want Galatea to come to life?*

Pyramus and Thisbe

The red berries of the mulberry tree were once white as snow. This tale of two lovers tells how the mulberries changed.

Pyramus and Thisbe lived in Babylon, a rich and splendid city. Pyramus was known as the most handsome young man in the land. Thisbe was said to be the most beautiful maiden.

Pyramus and Thisbe lived next door to each other. The time came when they fell in love. They wanted to marry, but a problem stood in their way. Their parents had quarreled once over some unimportant matter. They'd never gotten over their anger.

"You must not see Thisbe!" Pyramus's parents told him.

"Stay away from Pyramus!" said Thisbe's father and mother.

Pyramus and Thisbe did try to stay apart. But their love was too strong.

A brick wall separated the houses of the two families. One day the lovers discovered a hole in the wall. A single stone was missing. Pyramus and Thisbe began to steal away

Whispered words of love

from their houses. They secretly spoke to each other through the wall. Day after day they met and whispered words of love. But the hole was very small. It was too tiny to reach even a hand through. So Pyramus and Thisbe could share only words, never a touch.

At last the young lovers could stand it no longer. "We must meet somewhere!" Pyramus cried. "We must leave and go where we can be together!"

Thisbe agreed. She loved Pyramus more than life itself.

"But we must not leave Babylon together," Pyramus said. "Someone might see us and tell our parents."

Pyramus and Thisbe decided to see each other that night outside the city gates. They would meet near a spring under a tall mulberry tree. There they would not be seen. Few people went out of town at night. Most of them feared the wild animals that roamed the woods.

That night Thisbe waited until her household was asleep. She wrapped a silk cloak around herself and tiptoed away. She had no trouble getting out of the city. And she had no trouble finding the place Pyramus had described. A mulberry tree hung over a spring, its white berries gleaming in the moonlight. Thisbe pulled her cloak tighter about her. She sat down to wait for Pyramus.

Before long, Thisbe heard a rustling noise in the bushes.

"Pyramus?" she called.

But it was not her love who came out of the bushes. Instead, it was a large lion! The lion's jaws were dripping with blood. It had just killed some animal and was coming to the stream to drink.

Thisbe did not wait a second. She jumped up and ran. Her cloak fell from her shoulders. Thisbe did not dare to stop to pick it up. She ran until she came to a thick stand of trees. There she hid, shivering and crying with fear.

The lion was not hungry and had no interest in Thisbe. It drank from the stream.

Then it noticed Thisbe's cloak lying on the ground. The lion sniffed the cloak, pawed it, and bit it with blood-stained jaws. Then the lion turned away and went off into the woods.

Moments later Pyramus arrived. He was out of breath from running. His family had not gone to bed until very late. Oh, how he had worried about Thisbe waiting in the darkness!

"Thisbe?" he called softly as he neared the stream. "Thisbe?"

There was no answer. Pyramus looked about. He saw the lion's footprints in the mud by the stream. All color left his face. There was Thisbe's cloak! Pyramus picked it up. The cloak was torn and streaked with blood.

"No!" Pyramus cried. He turned his face to the heavens. "No!" he cried again. "Oh, Thisbe, I told you to come to this place. *I,* who wanted to love and protect you, have caused your death! I cannot live with that pain."

Then Pyramus took out his sword and plunged it into his body. He fell to the ground. His blood splashed onto the berries of the mulberry tree.

About this time, Thisbe was deciding to leave her hiding place. The lion must be gone by now, she thought. And surely Pyramus would be arriving. She crept back to the place she had left.

What is that? she wondered as she neared the spot. A form lay in the darkness near the stream. It was hard to see with only the moon for light. Was it the lion?

Then Thisbe saw something move. It looked like a human hand. It moved again. Thisbe ran forward. When she saw Pyramus, she screamed and fell to her knees beside him.

"What has happened?" she cried. "Answer me, Pyramus. It is I, your Thisbe."

At the sound of her name, Pyramus opened his eyes. His lips moved, but no words came from them. Pyramus closed his eyes again. He died in Thisbe's arms.

What could Thisbe do? Her love was dead. And since she had gone against her parents, they would never take her back. "How could this have happened?" she cried.

Then, looking about, Thisbe saw her torn cloak. She saw Pyramus's sword beside his body. Thisbe knew what had happened. "Your own hand killed you. That and your love for me. I love you, too, Pyramus." Thisbe took Pyramus's sword and drove it into her heart.

The parents of Thisbe and Pyramus buried their children in a single tomb.

The gods were sad. In honor of the lovers, they changed the mulberry tree. They turned its white berries red. The tree they had died under would be marked forever with Pyramus and Thisbe's blood.

1. *Why didn't the parents of Pyramus and Thisbe want them to see each other?*
2. *Why did Pyramus think Thisbe was dead?*
3. *What color were mulberries before Pyramus and Thisbe died?*

Jason and the Golden Fleece

Jason was born a prince. He should have become the king of Thessaly. But he gained his throne only after an adventure-filled journey.

The Man with One Sandal

The King of Thessaly was old and sick. He knew he would not live much longer. But his only son was much too young to rule a kingdom. Jason was just a baby. So the king went to his brother, Pelias.

"I can no longer rule," the king said. "Will you take the throne while Jason is a child? You must agree that my son will be king when he reaches manhood."

Pelias quickly agreed. But he was not a good man. He secretly decided that Jason would never be king. He, Pelias, would remain king of Thessaly for as long as he lived!

Not long after, the old king died. Immediately, Pelias ordered Jason sent far away. He should never learn that he was of royal blood. To be sure his future as king was safe, Pelias went to a fortune-teller. "What do you see ahead?" he asked.

The fortune-teller's only answer was, "Beware the man who wears one shoe."

Years went by. At first Pelias watched and waited for the man with one shoe. But as time passed, no such person appeared. Pelias stopped worrying. He forgot the fortune-teller's warning.

Meanwhile, Jason was growing up in a faraway land. He had no idea of his royalty. When it came time to go to school, Jason studied with the Centaurs. Now the Centaur was a strange creature. Above the waist, it was a man. Below the waist, it had the body of a horse. The Centaur had the wisdom of a man and the strength and speed of a horse. The Centaur was indeed an amazing creature.

Jason's special teacher was a Centaur named Chiron. When Chiron felt that Jason had finished his schooling, he took him aside. He told the young man about his true birth. "You are a king," Chiron said. "And the time has come for you to seek your throne. But be careful of King Pelias. He is tricky and will not give up easily."

Jason was brave and strong. He was ready to go to Thessaly and take the kingdom from Pelias. He barely heard Chiron's warning.

The trip to Thessaly was long and hard. As Jason neared the kingdom, he found his way blocked by a raging river. Many had tried, but no one had ever crossed its rushing waters. Jason would not be stopped. He stepped into the river. The swift current almost knocked him down, but he kept his feet. He was nearly across when a fallen tree hit him from behind. Jason was swept under and thrown against the rocks. It seemed he had disappeared. But then, there he was, pulling himself up out of the river.

Jason rested on the bank. He waited for his strength to return. Looking down, he saw that he had lost a sandal in the river. No matter, he thought. Soon he would be in Thessaly.

When King Pelias saw the tall young man standing in his doorway, his heart turned inside him. Jason was wearing only one sandal.

"Who are you, young stranger?" Pelias asked. He tried to sound calm.

"Uncle Pelias, I am Jason, rightful king of Thessaly. I have come to claim my throne."

"Jason!" Pelias cried. "My boy, you have come. We thought we had lost you. Oh, how we have hoped for your return." As he spoke, Pelias wondered how he could get rid of his nephew.

He came up with a plan. Pelias pretended to be happy to turn over the kingdom. "I am getting old," he said. "It is a welcome rest you offer me. But," Pelias said, "wouldn't you first like to have some adventure? Why, you're still young and full of spirit! Besides, we should show the people of Thessaly you're a hero. They will want to know you're worthy of the throne."

Jason was a high-spirited youth. Pelias could see he was interested. "Far away," Pelias said, "is a land called Colchis. There you will find a golden fleece. This fleece is the skin of a golden sheep. It once belonged to your family. Believe me, your people would think it most wonderful if you could bring it home."

"It sounds like a great adventure!" Jason cried. "But what about my kingdom?"

"I will be happy to watch over it until you return." Pelias knew the way to Colchis was dangerous. He also knew that the king of Colchis was a fierce warrior. He wouldn't give up the fleece. Pelias was sure Jason would never return alive.

1. *What is a fleece?*
2. *What did the fortune-teller warn Pelias about?*
3. *Why did Pelias really send Jason after the golden fleece?*

The Quest for the Golden Fleece

Jason went to see Argus, the finest shipbuilder in all of Greece. Argus built Jason a fine boat. It was large enough to hold many men. It was strong enough to pass through the roughest seas. Jason named the ship *Argo*.

Then Jason called for a contest. He asked the strongest and bravest men to test their skills. The winners would be invited to join him on his quest.

There were races, wrestling matches, and throwing contests. At last 50 winners stood before Jason. Among them was the famous hero Hercules. These 50 men would make up the *Argo*'s crew. Jason called them the Argonauts.

The *Argo* sailed from Thessaly on a beautiful morning. Not a cloud marked the blue sky. A fine breeze filled the ship's sails. People crowded the shore to wish the heroes a safe journey. They poured wine into the sea as an offering to the gods.

The goddess Hera smiled down on the Argonauts. And she whispered in Jason's ear. "Seek Phineas in the land of Thrace. He will help you as your journey begins."

So Jason set a course for Thrace. There they found Phineas. "Hera has sent me here,"

Jason told the old man. "Do you have some words of wisdom for my crew?"

Phineas told the Argonauts about two great rocks they had to pass through. When something came between them, the rocks clashed together with a terrible force. Anything caught there would be crushed.

"But I will teach you a trick," Phineas said. "As you near the rocks, set loose a dove. Let it fly before you. As it passes between the rocks, they will clash together to try to catch it. The dove will be too fast. It will escape. But be ready. Just as the rocks pull apart, you must row with all your might. With the help of the gods, you might get through before the rocks clash together again."

The sea grew dark as the *Argo* neared the rocks Phineas had described. Great waves pounded the ship from every side.

"There they are!" cried one of the Argonauts. Two huge rocks rose out of the sea like twin mountains. Even the bravest Argonauts gasped at the sight of them.

Jason set loose a dove. It flew straight ahead. Suddenly, a great roar filled the air. The rocks were moving. They quickly came together with a crash. But the little dove had been fast enough. Only her tailfeathers were caught between the towering rocks.

"To the oars!" ordered Jason. "Row for your lives!" The Argonauts pulled on the oars. Their muscles burned. Sweat stood out on their foreheads. The *Argo* shot forward between the great rocks. Only the boat's stern was grazed as the rocks came together.

On their voyage to Colchis, the heroes met other adventures. One man died while hunting a wild boar. Others died of sickness. The Argonauts were attacked by giant birds. They passed the island of women warriors known as Amazons. But at last they reached Colchis. There, Jason knew, they would find the golden fleece.

After the success of his journey, Jason was very sure of himself. "Wait on the ship until you hear from me," he told his men. He left the ship alone and went straight to Aeetes, the king of Colchis. Jason told Aeetes he had come for the golden fleece. It was rightly his, he said.

King Aeetes became very angry when he heard Jason's bold words. "Not so fast, young fellow," he said. "Did you think I would give you the fleece? It has long been in Colchis. It has brought us wealth and good fortune."

Then Aeetes got word of Jason's small but strong army of Argonauts. The king did not want war. "Indeed," he said, "if you really want the fleece, you may have it. But you must prove yourself worthy by performing two tasks.

"First," Aeetes went on, "you must go to my fields. There you will find two bulls. They were gifts to me from the god Ares. You must yoke the bulls to the plow. Then plant dragon's teeth in the field. But beware the crop that grows from those seeds!"

Aeetes led Jason to the field. There Jason saw two huge bulls. Their hooves were made of bronze. Their red eyes rolled angrily in their heads. They pawed the ground. Flames shot out of their mouths. Smoke curled from their noses. How would Jason ever get close enough to the animals? He'd be burned to death.

"Tomorrow," the king said, "you will begin your tasks."

Jason couldn't sleep that night. The job Aeetes had set before him was too great. In the middle of his worrying, Jason heard knocking. He opened his door to find a beautiful woman. She was Medea, daughter of King Aeetes. Jason had seen her earlier that day. She'd been sitting silently at her father's side. Medea's dark beauty had caught Jason's eye. Yet something about her looked strange and dangerous to him.

Medea slipped into the room. She closed the door behind her. She told Jason that with one glance she had fallen in love with him.

"No mortal man can perform the tasks my father has given you," Medea said. "But I have many powers and can help you. Promise to marry me, Jason. Take me with you. I will help you gain the golden fleece."

Jason did not love the girl, but she was very beautiful. And he could see no other way to get the fleece. He agreed.

Medea gave Jason a magic herb. "Use this on the bulls. They will become tame as lambs."

Then she gave him a black stone. "This, too, will help you in your quest."

Next morning, Jason followed the king to his fields. He walked toward the fire-breathing bulls. The bulls roared and charged. But Jason did not back away. Instead, he held out the magic herb Medea had given him. When the bulls got a whiff of the herb, they stopped their charge. They stood whimpering like puppies as Jason slipped the yoke over their heads. King Aeetes watched angrily as Jason plowed his field.

"You have completed the first task," the king said when Jason had finished. "Now plant these seeds." Aeetes handed Jason a helmet filled with dragon's teeth.

Jason took the helmet and walked up and down the field. He scattered the seeds and then stood back. The ground began to tremble.

Jason's first task

Imagine Jason's surprise as the seeds began to sprout their terrible crop. From each seed a fierce soldier grew. They wore shiny helmets and carried long, sharp spears. These children of the dragon's teeth had risen to kill whoever had planted their seeds.

The soldiers began a steady march toward Jason. He could never fight so many! Then he remembered the black stone Medea had given him. He threw the stone into the advancing line of soldiers.

Clank! The stone hit a soldier's helmet. The soldier turned to the man nearest him and struck him with his spear. His angry neighbor struck back. Soon the soldiers born of the dragon's teeth were fighting among themselves. Jason was forgotten. The soldiers fought one another until not one of them was left alive.

King Aeetes buried his head in his hands. He roared with anger.

"Quickly! Follow me!" Medea cried to Jason. Medea knew her father would never give away the golden fleece. She knew he'd put Jason and the Argonauts to death.

Medea ran into the woods. Jason followed her to a clearing. "The fleece is there," Medea whispered. She pointed to a large tree. Jason looked up and saw the glittering sheepskin.

Jason started forward, but he jumped back quickly. For a dreadful dragon was coming out of the woods. It switched its tail and turned its head from side to side.

"He guards the fleece night and day," Medea said. "He never sleeps. Don't think you are the first to come after the golden fleece. All others have failed." She pointed to a pile of bones that lay before the tree.

Then Medea reached into her robe and brought out a small bottle. "Here," she said to Jason. "Use this magic potion. Just a few drops of it will put the dragon to sleep."

Jason sprinkled the magic potion on the ground as he approached the dragon. Within seconds, the beast collapsed and fell fast asleep. Jason quickly drew out his sword and cut off the dragon's head. Then he pulled the golden fleece from the tree. He took Medea's hand, and they headed for Jason's ship. Aeetes and his army would soon be after them.

"Hurry!" Jason shouted to his crew as he boarded the ship. Aeetes and his men were already at the shore. "Make sail!"

The Argonauts stared in surprise at the beautiful dark-haired woman who'd just come aboard. But they quickly did as Jason had ordered them to do. A stiff wind caught the sails, and the *Argo* was off.

4. *What trick did Jason use to row the boat safely through the crashing rocks?*

5. *What did Aeetes tell Jason to plant in the field? What grew from them?*

6. *What did Medea give Jason to help him with the bulls?*

The Hero Returns

The Argonauts had some exciting moments on their voyage home. But with the goddess Hera's help and Medea's magic, they arrived safely in Thessaly.

When Jason returned, the people greeted him as a great hero. "When shall I be crowned king?" Jason asked Pelias.

"Soon," Pelias answered. "But the people are not very fond of your new queen. She comes from another land. They don't trust her. Give them time to get to know her better. Then you shall have the crown."

Time passed. Pelias kept finding reasons to remain on the throne. Medea saw that Pelias was the enemy. But she could not convince Jason. She decided at last to take matters into her own hands.

Medea went to Pelias's two daughters. She offered to teach them magic spells. She killed an old goat before their eyes. Then she sprinkled herbs on it and said some magic words. The animal sprang back to life as a frisky young lamb.

"Will it work on people, too?" asked one of the daughters. She was thinking of Pelias. He was getting very old.

"Of course," answered Medea. "With these herbs and the magic words, you can make anyone young again." She gave the two girls the herbs and went away. She was quite sure what would happen next.

Indeed, the two silly girls murdered their own father. Then they sprinkled his body with the herbs. They chanted and chanted. But unlike the goat, Pelias did not return to life. When the sisters looked for Medea, they found she had left the city. Medea was afraid to remain after what she had done.

Jason became king. But soon afterward he followed his queen to Corinth. There they had two sons. At times Medea missed her father and her home in Colchis. Still, she did have Jason. He eased her loneliness.

In time, however, Jason grew tired of Medea. He decided he wanted to marry the young princess of Corinth. He forgot all that Medea had done for him. He offered her gold and asked her to go away.

The fury that Medea felt would have

frightened the bravest mortal. She thought about the way she had gone against her own father for Jason. She had played wicked tricks and left her home. Now she would punish Jason. And she knew just how to do it.

Medea took from among her things a lovely robe trimmed with jewels. She rubbed the robe with a deadly poison. Then she sent it in a beautiful box to the princess of Corinth.

When the princess opened the box, she shouted with delight. "Who could have sent such a gift?" she wondered aloud. She lifted the robe from the box and put it on. She paraded up and down the room feeling the soft cloth on her shoulders. Then her skin suddenly began to burn. The princess felt weak. She pulled at the robe, but it would not come off. Within moments, the princess fell to the floor. She was dead.

When Jason found her, he knew exactly who was to blame. He rushed from the palace in search of Medea. In the streets of Corinth, he looked up and saw her on the roof of a house. She was just stepping into a chariot drawn by flying dragons.

"Look what you have done, Jason," she called. "You made me turn against my father and my country. You took me to a strange land. I killed for you. And you left me for another

Medea leaves Jason

woman. I fear you will take out your anger on our sons. I could not let them live under such a threat. You will find them dead. I, who gave them life, have given them death. Now you, too, have lost your family!"

With those words, Medea flew into the air in her chariot. She left Jason behind. He was no longer a hero. He was now a man who had lost everything.

7. *How did Medea trick Pelias's daughters?*

8. *What did Medea send to the princess of Corinth? Why?*

9. *Where did Jason find Medea? What had she done?*

Perseus and the Gorgon's Head

The gods declared that the king of Argos would one day be killed by his own grandson. The king could not escape his fate. But in trying to do so, he sent his grandson Perseus on some dangerous adventures.

The king of Argos had only one child, a daughter named Danae. She was very beautiful and very sweet. But the king wanted a son. He asked the gods if he would ever have one. The answer they gave was not what the king wanted to hear.

"You shall have no son. But your daughter, Danae, shall give you a grandson. Beware, for your daughter's son will one day kill you."

The king decided he would outsmart the gods. He would keep Danae from ever becoming a mother! He had a house built deep beneath the earth. Only a small shaft was open to the sky to let in light and air. The king locked his daughter away in this house. There, he said, she must spend the rest of her life.

Danae was lonely and sad. The god Zeus felt sorry for her. One night he visited the beautiful girl. Zeus came down the air shaft beautiful girl. Zeus came down the air shaft in a shower of golden rain. He spent the whole night with Danae.

The king soon found that his plan had not worked. The Princess Danae bore a child by Zeus. She called the boy Perseus.

The king was frightened. He was sure this was the child who would one day kill him. The king would have put the child to death immediately. But he was afraid such an act would anger the gods. So he had a great chest made out of wood and brass. He shut his daughter and her baby inside the chest and cast them into the sea. Surely, the king thought, they would drown or starve.

But the gods watched over Danae and Perseus. The chest washed up on the shore of a faraway island. A kind fisherman named Dictys found the chest and its strange contents. He took the princess and her son home. For many years, he took care of them. Perseus grew into a handsome young man. And in contests of strength, he could beat anyone on the island.

As time passed, Danae fell in love with the fisherman who had saved her. Now Dictys happened to be the brother of the ruler of the island. King Polydectes was as harsh and cruel as Dictys was kind and gentle. Polydectes had noticed Danae's beauty. He wanted her for his wife. But he knew he could never take her as long as Perseus was around to protect her. So he figured out a plan to get rid of him.

King Polydectes invited all the young men of the island to a feast. As was the custom, each guest brought the king a present. But Perseus was poor. He had no gift. So Perseus stood up before Polydectes and said, "I offer you my courage and my skill."

This was exactly what the king hoped Perseus would say. "Go then, Perseus," the king said. "Prove your courage. Bring me the head of Medusa the Gorgon. This would be the best gift of all!"

Everyone at the feast gasped. This was an impossible task! No one who had set eyes on the Gorgons had lived! The king was plotting Perseus's death!

The Gorgons were three hideous sisters. They lived on a rocky island. Below their waists, they looked like dragons with hard sharp scales. Above their waists, they looked like women. But instead of hair, they had snakes slithering about their heads. Medusa was the most frightful of the three. Whoever looked at her was turned to stone.

But Perseus had offered his services to the king. He knew he had to keep his word. So he set out to find Medusa.

Fortunately, two great gods were watching over Perseus. Hermes and Athena would help him perform his impossible task. Athena lent him her bright shield. It shone like a mirror. She also gave him a magic bag. This bag grew in size to hold anything that was put into it. Hermes gave Perseus his winged sandals. With them, Perseus could fly through the air. Hermes also gave him a sword. It was strong enough to cut through the Gorgon's scales. Last of all, the gods gave Perseus a magic cap. This would make him invisible.

The gods sent Perseus to the end of the world to visit the three Gray Women. They alone knew where to find the Gorgon. The Gray Women were strange creatures who shared one eye among them. They took turns using it. One would look about with the eye placed in the middle of her forehead. Then she'd take it out and pass it to one of her sisters.

"You must steal the eye," Hermes told Perseus. "It is the only way to get the sisters to tell you where to find the Gorgons."

Perseus followed Hermes's advice. He found the strange old women and hid behind them. He listened to them argue among themselves.

"Give me the eye!" one cried.

"No, it's still my turn!" shouted another.

"I want the eye next!" the third one said.

As one tried to snatch the eye from the other, Perseus sprang forward. He grabbed it. "You can have your eye back," he said, "when you tell me where to find the Gorgons."

When he had the directions, Perseus returned the eye. Then he flew away on Hermes's winged sandals. Near the Gorgons' island, he heard the hissing of snakes.

Perseus did not look directly down at the Gorgons. He knew that if he did he would turn to stone. He floated above them, looking into Athena's bright shield. It acted like a mirror. In it, he could see the dreadful Gorgons. All three were asleep. But the snakes on their heads wriggled and hissed and darted their tongues. Still looking into the shield, Perseus swooped low. With one quick slash of Hermes's sword, he struck off Medusa's head. He picked it up and dropped it into the magic bag.

Medusa's sisters woke up and saw their dead sister. Screaming and shrieking, they tried to grab Perseus with their sharp claws. But Perseus put on the magic cap of darkness and disappeared.

Perseus had other adventures on his way home. In one, he saved the life of a beautiful young maiden named Andromeda. Perseus married Andromeda and with her sailed back to his mother.

But Perseus found that things were not well in the kingdom of Polydectes. His mother, Danae, had been treated cruelly by the king. She had refused to marry him. Both Danae and Dictys had hidden in a temple to escape the king's rage.

The angry Perseus marched straight to the king's castle. He found Polydectes feasting with many of his friends. When Perseus entered the dining hall, Polydectes grew pale.

"Ah, Perseus!" he cried. "You have come back without the head you promised me."

"You asked me for Medusa's head," said Perseus. "Now, behold it!" Perseus pulled the Gorgon's head from the magic bag. Keeping his own eyes turned away, he held it high before the king. With that, Polydectes and his friends turned to stone.

The people of the island were happy. Polydectes had been a harsh ruler. His brother, the kind fisherman Dictys, became king. Danae became queen.

As for Perseus, he decided to return to the island of his birth. On his way back to Argos, Perseus stopped to rest in another kingdom. A great sporting contest was being held there. Perseus was proud of his skill and strength. He decided to enter a discus-throwing contest.

Polydectes meets Medusa

When his turn came, Perseus threw the discus so hard it flew into the crowd. Perseus was shocked to learn that the discus had killed a visiting king. He was even more shocked to learn that the dead man was his own grandfather! The king of Argos did meet his death at the hands of his grandson. He had not escaped his fate.

This was the last of Perseus's problems. He and Andromeda went on to Argos. There they ruled happily as king and queen.

1. Why did the king lock up Danae?
2. What happened to anyone who looked at Medusa?
3. How did Perseus get the Gray Women to tell him where the Gorgons were?

Theseus and the Minotaur

Theseus saved Athens from having to send its sons and daughters to their deaths.

The Road to Athens

At one time, the good king Aegeus ruled Athens. When traveling far from home, King Aegeus fell in love with a beautiful princess named Aethra. The two married, and they spent some time in Aethra's land. They had a son there whom they named Theseus.

One day, a message arrived. It called King Aegeus back to Athens. His kingdom had been attacked by the armies of King Minos of Crete.

"You must stay here, my love," Aegeus told Aethra. "I do not know how long this war in Athens will last."

Before the king left, he led his queen to the top of a hill. There King Aegeus dug a hole. In it he buried a sword and a pair of sandals. Then he rolled a huge rock over the hole.

"Someday," Aegeus said, "our son will be strong enough to lift this stone. He will take the sword and sandals for himself. On that day, you must send him to me."

So Theseus was raised by his mother. Aethra made sure he learned to run and jump, and to wrestle and box. Theseus became the strongest boy in the land.

But Aethra knew there were things just as important as strength. She taught her son to love music and poetry. She made sure visitors told Theseus of faraway kingdoms. He learned about good and evil in the world.

One day Aethra looked closely at her son. She saw his tall handsome frame. She saw his steady blue eyes. "Come with me," she said quietly. Taking his hand, she led Theseus to the hilltop.

"Lift that stone for me," she said at the top of the grassy hill.

Young Theseus bent down and put both hands around the huge stone. Without much effort, he lifted it and moved it aside. Theseus was surprised to see the sandals and sword in the shallow hole.

He looked at his mother. Her eyes were bright with pride. But they were also marked with sadness. "The time has come," Aethra said. Then she told Theseus all about his father, the king of Athens. "You must go to your father. Take this sword and wear these sandals. He has left them for you. A ship will be ready in the morning."

Theseus lifted the sword. "I will go, Mother," he said in a firm voice. "But I will not travel by sea. That route is too safe and easy. I will go overland. Perhaps I can prove myself worthy of being the son of the king of Athens."

"It's too dangerous!" his mother cried. "There are wild beasts and thieves on the roads. You will be killed!" But Aethra couldn't talk Theseus out of traveling to Athens by land.

The next day, Theseus set off. His mother had been right. Soon enough he met a frightful-looking fellow on the road. The man had a huge muscular upper body. He had a large head and an ugly face. But his legs were small and thin and seemed barely able to carry the rest of him. This man turned out to be a robber. He had, in fact, killed many travelers with his gigantic club. He was no match, however, for young Theseus. Theseus took the robber's club away from him. Theseus raised the club high and then smashed the man's head in.

The story of the fearsome robber's death spread quickly. And Theseus had other adventures on the road to Athens. Each proved him to be a hero worthy of great praise. By the time he arrived in Athens, Theseus was known throughout the land.

King Aegeus invited Theseus to a feast in his honor. But the king didn't know Theseus was his son. He had fallen under the power of Medea, a woman who could cast spells.

Because she had special powers, Medea knew Theseus was the king's child. But she feared she'd lose her power over Aegeus if he found out.

"This stranger who calls himself a hero is trying to trick you," she whispered to Aegeus. "He will try to take your throne. We must get rid of him. Give him this cup of poisoned wine. Only then will your kingdom be safe."

Under Medea's spell, Aegeus agreed to give Theseus the wine. That night, he handed his only son a golden cup filled with poison. But before Theseus drank from it, the king saw the jeweled sword he wore. Then Aegeus knew who Theseus was. The king grabbed the cup and threw it to the ground. He hugged his son, and tears of joy streamed from his eyes.

Medea then fled the kingdom and was never seen there again.

1. *For whom did King Aegeus bury a sword and a pair of sandals?*

2. *Why didn't Theseus want to travel to his father by sea?*

3. *How did Aegeus discover Theseus's true identity?*

The Minotaur

King Aegeus was indeed happy that his son had come to Athens. But there was trouble in his kingdom. Minos, the ruler of Crete, had won the war that Aegeus had gone home to fight. Now the people of Athens had to pay King Minos a terrible price.

"It happens every year," Aegeus told his son. "We must send seven of our finest young men and seven of our most beautiful maidens to the island of Crete. There King Minos sacrifices them to a terrible monster. It is half man and half beast. Minos calls this monster the Minotaur. The time has come again. We must now send our own people to meet their deaths in Crete."

When Theseus heard this, he knew he had come to Athens at the right time. "I will go to Crete, Father. I will go as one of the sacrifices. But I will put an end to this!"

"No one can stop the Minotaur!" cried Aegeus. "King Minos keeps the beast in the middle of a great maze. The maze was built by Daedalus. And no one who has ever gone in has found the way out. Minos sends his victims into the maze without weapons. Within its passages, the Minotaur finds them, and it eats them! Theseus, if you go to Crete, that will be your fate!"

The king begged Theseus to stay with him in Athens. "Oh, my son," King Aegeus cried, "no one escapes the Minotaur! I have only just found you. Please don't ask me to send you to your death!"

But Theseus was determined to go. He sailed away with six young men and seven young women. They traveled in a small ship with a black sail.

"I will pray for your return," King Aegeus said. "I will wait and watch."

"We will come back safely," said Theseus. "On the trip home, we will change this black sail to a white sail. It will be a signal. When you see us returning, you will know we have good news."

A crowd had gathered when the 14 Athenians arrived in Crete. In the crowd was Princess Ariadne, daughter of King Minos. The moment she saw Theseus, so tall and brave, she fell in love. She decided she couldn't let such a handsome young man, who walked like a king, die in the maze.

The guards led the Athenians to a cold dungeon. They threw Theseus into a small dark cell by himself. Late that night, Theseus heard the cell door creak open. He looked up to see the figure of a woman in the dim light. Her golden hair seemed to brighten the darkness. Her bare feet made no noise on the stone floor. It was Ariadne.

"Quickly," she whispered. "You must come with me if you want to live."

Ariadne led Theseus out of the dungeon. They went to the great maze Daedalus had built for King Minos.

There Ariadne held out a sword and a ball of silken thread. "Take this sword to fight the Minotaur," she said to Theseus. "The thread will be your means of escape if you can slay the beast. As you enter the maze, tie one end of it to a pillar. Unwind the thread as you walk. Then you will be able to follow the thread back to the entrance."

"But why have you done this for me?" Theseus asked before entering the maze. He found it hard to take his eyes off Ariadne's beautiful face. Ariadne said nothing. But Theseus read the answer in her eyes.

"I will slay the Minotaur," he declared. "Wait for me here."

Theseus entered the maze. He unwound the ball of thread as he moved forward. Ariadne could hear his footsteps echoing against the walls for a while. But the sound grew fainter as Theseus went farther into the maze. Then Ariadne heard a fierce roar from deep within.

Theseus found the Minotaur lying on the ground. His shaggy head swayed to the left and right as he looked about him. The beast was twice as large as any man Theseus had ever seen. He had the head of a gigantic bull. The Minotaur roared and sprang for Theseus as soon as he spotted him. But Theseus was ready. He thrust his sword at the monster and wounded him. The angry beast sprang again at Theseus. This time Theseus's sword found the Minotaur's heart. The earth shook as the great creature fell. Theseus then followed Ariadne's silken thread to the maze's entrance.

Ariadne and Theseus rushed back to the dungeon. They set free the other Athenian men and women. Then they all hurried to the ship.

"You must sail with me," Theseus said to Ariadne. "You will not be safe in Crete when your father learns you helped me. Come with me to Athens. Be my wife, Ariadne."

On the trip home, Theseus's ship stopped on a small island to make some repairs. Somehow, Ariadne wandered off. Theseus searched for Ariadne, but he could not find her.

"We must go!" cried the ship's crew. They were worried that King Minos's armies would come after them. "We can wait no longer!" they insisted. Theseus had to leave the island without Ariadne.

The god Dionysus found Ariadne alone on the tiny island. Seeing her great beauty, he took her to Mount Olympus to be his bride.

While the crew cheered their escape, Theseus sat alone on the deck of the ship. His grief over the loss of his love chased all thought from his mind. Theseus forgot to change the ship's sail. The ship neared Athens still powered by the black sail.

King Aegeus had been waiting for the ship to return. Each day he watched from a rock high above the sea. On the day he saw the black sail, he thought his son was dead. Aegeus then felt he could no longer live. He threw himself into the ocean. The waters he leapt to were forever after known as the Aegean Sea.

Theseus's homecoming was a sad one. But he became king and showed unusual kindness. Theseus let his subjects choose the laws they would follow. Some say he even gave up the title of king and let the people of Athens rule.

4. *What was the Minotaur? Where was it kept?*

5. *How did Theseus find his way out of the maze?*

6. *What did King Aegeus think when he saw the black sail?*

The 12 Labors of Hercules

One of the greatest heroes was half man and half god. His Greek name was Heracles. He became better known by his Roman name, Hercules.

Young Hercules

Hercules was different from other children. His mother discovered early that Hercules was very, very strong. But this wasn't the only thing that set Hercules apart. Although his mother was a mortal, Hercules's father was a god. In fact, Zeus was the most powerful god on Mount Olympus.

Zeus watched over Hercules. But from the day Hercules was born, Hera was jealous and angry. Hera was Zeus's wife on Mount Olympus. And she planned to make trouble for Hercules all the days of his life.

When Hercules was still a baby, Hera sent two deadly snakes to his room. She hoped they would kill the sleeping child. But Hercules woke up. He grabbed one snake in each chubby hand and strangled them both. From then on, everyone knew Hercules would be a hero.

As a boy, Hercules worked in the mountains herding sheep. One day a lion came upon the herd. He was looking for something to eat. Hercules killed that lion with his bare hands. He skinned the beast and wore its skin as a cloak.

Hercules grew into a fine young man. He was stronger, it seemed, than any man on earth. He could wrestle and run and throw a spear. A king offered his daughter to Hercules as a wife. Hercules married the lovely young woman. They had three children.

The family lived happily until Hera cast a terrible madness upon Hercules. Without knowing what he was doing, Hercules killed his wife and children. When he came to his senses, he saw what he had done.

"How can I live with this?" he cried. "How can I ever be free of the pain I feel?"

The gods sent Hercules a message. "You must go to Mycenae and serve King Eurystheus for 12 years. Only then will you be free of your pain and guilt."

King Eurystheus was a weak and cowardly man. He was jealous of Hercules's great strength. Eurystheus was happy to make the strong man work hard. Hera joined forces with the king. Together they came up with 12 difficult tasks for Hercules. The tasks sent the hero on 12 great adventures. These adventures became known as the 12 labors of Hercules.

1. *Why was Hera so jealous of Hercules?*
2. *Why did Hercules have to go to Mycenae?*
3. *Who helped King Eurystheus come up with 12 tasks for Hercules?*

The First Three Labors

"You must kill the lion of Nemea!" the king told Hercules. "That is your first task."

For years this terrible lion had roamed the countryside. He had killed a few people and frightened many. Great hunters had tried to capture the beast. All had failed.

Hercules made his way to the lion's valley. There he found empty farmyards and fields. Everyone was so afraid that they were staying in their houses.

Hercules heard a rustling in some nearby bushes. He stood as still as a statue. The great lion walked into his sight. Its huge face was streaked with blood, for it had just eaten. Hercules calmly fit an arrow into his bow. He drew back the bow and released the arrow. It flew straight to the great beast's chest. But the

Hercules returns to the king

arrow did not go in. It bounced right off the lion. Again Hercules shot an arrow. Again it bounced to the ground. Before Hercules could shoot a third arrow, the lion sprang for him. Hercules struck the lion with his heavy club. The club broke in two over the lion's head.

Now Hercules was without weapons. There was nothing he could do but wrestle the lion. Hercules grabbed the beast and wrapped his arms around its neck. The lion roared. It reared up and clawed the air. Hercules squeezed the lion's neck tighter and tighter. The lion thrashed about until its strength was gone. At last the fight was over. The lion was dead.

Hercules tossed the dead animal over his shoulder. He carried it back to the city. When the king saw Hercules, he trembled in fear of his strength. And the king became angry because Hercules had made him feel such fear. "The next task," the king said to Hera, "must be an impossible one!"

As a second task, the king sent Hercules to a dark swamp. There lived a snakelike monster called the Hydra. The Hydra had nine heads. One of these heads could never die. The other eight were also magical. If one were cut off, the Hydra grew two more in its place.

Hercules had a plan. But he knew he'd need help. He asked Iolaus to go with him.

Hercules and his nephew found the Hydra slithering about in the swamp. Its nine mouths snarled and hissed. Its poisonous breath filled the air. Hercules began hacking at the heads with his sword. But every time he cut one off, two grew back to strike out at him.

"Now, Iolaus!" Hercules cried. Iolaus rushed forward with a burning torch. Each time Hercules cut off a head, Iolaus pushed the torch into the Hydra's wound. The heat kept new heads from growing. At last, Hercules had chopped off all the Hydra's heads. Only the one that would not die could hurt him. Hercules buried that head under a giant rock.

Hercules stood back and looked at the battle scene. The ground was all torn up. Trees had been blackened by the flaming torch. Hercules took out his arrows and dipped their tips into the Hydra's poisonous blood. Then he and Iolaus returned to Mycenae.

King Eurystheus was disappointed that Hercules had returned alive. He thought hard. What could he demand of Hercules now?

As a third task, the king sent Hercules to capture a beautiful golden deer. This was not a dangerous task. But it would be very difficult.

The deer had long golden horns. It was a favorite of the goddess Artemis. Hercules tracked the deer for a whole year. Sometimes at night he would see the creature. Its golden horns glittered in the moonlight. But swift as he was, Hercules could never catch it. He decided he would first have to wound it.

As soon as Hercules shot the deer with an arrow, Artemis appeared. "How dare you harm my beautiful deer!" she cried.

Hercules begged Artemis to forgive him. He swore he did not wish to kill the creature. He promised he would let it go after showing it to the king. Artemis believed Hercules. She let him take the golden deer to Eurystheus.

When Hercules appeared with the deer, the king was once more disappointed. He decided to plan something really dangerous for Hercules's fourth labor.

4. What were the first three labors?
5. How did Hercules keep new heads from growing on the Hydra?
6. What did Hercules finally have to do to catch the deer?

The Fourth, Fifth, and Sixth Labors

"A wild boar has been terrorizing the people who live on the mountainside. For your fourth labor, you must bring the boar back alive!"

Eurystheus rubbed his hands together and smiled. Hercules might be able to catch the wild boar. But he could never bring it alive and struggling back to the city.

Hercules went off on his mission. The king sat down to a feast.

Hercules found the boar in its cave. It was huge and ugly. It had sharp pointed tusks and short heavy legs. Stiff hairs bristled from its body. The boar snorted and puffed. Hercules attacked with his spear and club. The beast ran, and Hercules chased it and chased it. He drove it high up the mountain into the snow. At last the boar tired and fell into a deep snow bank. Hercules lifted the beast to his shoulders and carried it back to Mycenae.

King Eurystheus looked out the castle window and saw Hercules coming. The great beast was slung over his back. The boar was thrashing and growling now. Eurystheus realized that Hercules would bring the boar to him. The king was so frightened he ran and hid. It was days before he came out.

While he was in hiding, Eurystheus thought about Hercules's fifth labor. What would be hard enough for such a man? Eurystheus came up with a job that wasn't really dangerous. But it was disgusting.

"Go clean out the stables of King Augeas. You have one day to complete the job."

Now this may not sound like a very hard task. But it was really quite impossible. The Augean stables were the home of thousands of cattle. And the stables hadn't been cleaned in 30 years! When Hercules saw the mess, he knew one man couldn't do the job in a day.

Then Hercules saw two rivers running near the stable. He got an idea. Using all his great strength, Hercules dug ditches and built dams. He lifted huge logs and moved giant rocks. He changed the course of the rivers so that they flowed right through the stables. Their swift waters washed away the dirt of 30 years. Then Hercules knocked down his dams. He filled in his ditches. The rivers then returned to their natural course.

The sixth task given Hercules was chasing away the evil birds that lived at Stymphalus Lake. These birds had great claws and sharp curving beaks made of brass. They hid in the reeds beside the lake's dark waters. The birds ate anything, man or beast, that came along. No one had been able to stop them. Hercules took his bow and arrows and went to the lake.

At first Hercules was a bit worried. There were thousands of the fierce birds. And

Hercules saw that they could shoot their sharp feathers like arrows.

"Well," he thought, "let the fight begin." Hercules clanged a bell loudly to frighten the birds from their nests. The birds rose into the air, shooting their feathers. Hercules protected himself with his shield. For miles around, people heard the screeching of the birds and the clash of their feathers against Hercules's shield. Then Hercules shot his poisoned arrows into the sky. Not one missed its mark. The birds began falling into the lake. At last the few that hadn't been hit turned and flew out to sea. Stymphalus Lake was safe. And half the labors of the hero Hercules were completed.

7. *Why was cleaning the stables so hard?*

8. *How did Hercules change the course of a river?*

9. *What were the beaks of the birds at Stymphalus Lake made of?*

The Seventh, Eighth, and Ninth Labors

Hercules still had to complete six more tasks for King Eurystheus. Only then would he be free of his pain and guilt.

"There is a great bull on the island of

Crete," said King Eurystheus. "It was sent to earth by the sea god Poseidon. It sprang from the sea foam fully grown. Its color is snow-white. The bull has gone mad, and no one on the island is safe. You must bring me that bull, Hercules."

When Hercules arrived on Crete, he found the great bull pawing the ground. It tossed huge chunks of earth into the air with its silvery horns. Its sea-blue eyes gleamed with fury. There were no people on the plains near the bull. They had all run off in fear.

But Hercules was not afraid. He grabbed the bull by its horns and twisted hard. The beast roared in pain and fell to its knees. It turned and bucked its head, trying to force Hercules to let go. But the hero held on tightly.

When the bull saw that Hercules was its master, it became calm. Hercules brought the bull back to the king. He showed the tamed animal to Eurystheus. Then he let it go.

Eurystheus lost no time in sending Hercules off on another adventure. The eighth labor the king gave to him was capturing the man-eating horses that lived in Thrace. The people of Thrace were fierce and warlike. It was said that their king fed his horses on human flesh.

Hercules found the king's stables littered with human bones. Four horses had just finished dinner. Hercules took the horses by their manes and led them out of the stables. They bucked and reared. But Hercules was too strong for them. The stable hands were amazed at the hero's great strength. They stood aside and did not try to stop him. Hercules could have gotten away if the king hadn't come out then to see what was going on.

"What is all this noise?" the king bellowed.

When he saw Hercules taking his horses, he rushed at him. Hercules pushed the king aside. The king fell at his horses' feet. The hungry animals ate him.

Under Hercules's control, the horses quickly became tame. He led them back to Mycenae.

"Nothing will ever kill Hercules!" Eurystheus decided. "The best I can do is send him away for a long, long time."

So Eurystheus sent Hercules to the faraway country of the Amazons. The Amazons were a fierce tribe of warrior women. They were great archers and great fighters. Hippolyta, the queen of the Amazons, wore a beautiful golden belt. It had been given to her by Ares, the god of war. Eurystheus told

Hercules to bring him the belt. "My daughter," the king said, "would love to wear it."

For this ninth task, Hercules had to find himself a ship and crew. After a long and dangerous journey, they reached the land of the Amazons. At first, everything was fine. Hippolyta admired courage and strength. She greeted Hercules warmly. Hippolyta even gave Hercules her golden belt as a gift of friendship.

But Hera would not let things go well for Hercules. She disguised herself as an Amazon and went among the other women. "He is stealing our queen from us!" she whispered. "He will make her his prisoner!"

The women attacked Hercules. They thought they were protecting their queen. There was a terrible fight. The women were fierce warriors. Many of Hercules's men were killed. But when the fighting was over, all the Amazon women had been killed or frightened away. The body of Queen Hippolyta lay on the shore. Hercules sailed away with the golden belt. But he was very sad over the death of his new friend.

10. What god sent the bull to Crete?

11. Why did the horses eat their master?

12. Who made the Amazons attack Hercules?

The Tenth, Eleventh, and Twelfth Labors

For his tenth labor, Hercules had to face a very fierce-looking monster. Eurystheus sent him to an island where there lived the monster called Geryon. From the waist down, Geryon had the body of a single man. But from the waist up, he was three men. Geryon had three heads and six arms.

Geryon kept a herd of cattle. They were guarded by a two-headed dog and a giant. "Bring me the cattle of Geryon!" the king ordered Hercules.

Hercules sailed to the island. He found the cattle, along with the dog and the giant who were guarding them. Hercules fought both guardians with his mighty club. Then he herded the cattle together.

He was preparing to drive them onto his ship when the monster Geryon appeared. The hair on Geryon's three heads stood straight up in rage. His six eyes flashed. "Stop!" roared his three mouths. Hercules did not try to wrestle this monster. Instead, he shot him with one of his poisoned arrows.

Hercules traveled home with the cattle. The trip was full of dangers. At one point, Hercules stopped on land to rest. There he had to fight a fire-breathing giant who tried to steal some of the herd. Hercules did at last get most of the cattle to the king.

For his eleventh labor, Hercules had to fetch the apples of the Hesperides. The Hesperides were three nymphs who watched over some very special apples. Long ago, at the wedding of Hera and Zeus, everyone had brought gifts. The Earth gave the bride trees that bore apples of solid gold. The Hesperides now guarded those golden apples. A many-headed dragon helped them keep watch.

Most mortals had heard of the apples. But no one seemed to know just where they grew. Hercules traveled to many lands. He asked, "Where is the garden of the Hesperides?" But no one could tell him.

At last he decided to seek Atlas, the giant. He was the father of the Hesperides. Hercules found Atlas holding the weight of the skies on his shoulders. He asked the giant about the garden of the Hesperides.

"Yes, I know the place," Atlas answered. "And you can never go there. No mortal is allowed in the garden. But here, hold up the sky for me. I will go to the garden and get the apples for you."

Hercules bent over. He let Atlas shift the weight of the skies onto his own back. Atlas went off. Hercules waited for him to return. He waited and waited for what seemed to be a very long time. The skies got heavy on Hercules's back. But at last Atlas returned. In his hand, he held three glittering apples. "Stay a little longer," Atlas said. "I will take the apples to Eurystheus for you."

Hercules could see that Atlas was trying to trick him. The giant had grown tired of holding up the skies. He was trying to give the job to Hercules. But Hercules tricked Atlas instead.

"Take back the skies for just a moment before you go," Hercules said. "I want to make a pad to put on my shoulders. It will make the weight easier to bear."

Atlas was strong but not very smart. He put down the apples and took back the skies. Hercules quickly picked up the golden apples and left.

The twelfth labor of Hercules proved to be the most terrible of all. "Go down to the land of the dead," Eurystheus ordered. "Bring back Cerberus, the three-headed dog who watches over Hades's gate."

Hades was the god of the underworld. Eurystheus hoped Hades was strong enough to keep Hercules trapped forever.

So Hercules went off to the river Styx. He asked the ferryman to take him across to the land of the dead.

Cerberus, watchdog of the dead

Once he had crossed over, Hercules went straight down to the castle of Hades. He found Hades sitting in a dark hall. Beside him sat Persephone, his pale queen. Hercules asked Hades if he could carry Cerberus up to King Eurystheus. He told the god he had been ordered to do so. Hercules said he would then let the dog go.

Hades told Hercules he could take the dog. But he couldn't use any weapons to do it.

Hercules went to the front gates. There he found the frightful dog lying in the shadows. It growled as Hercules approached. He seized the beast by two of its throats. The third head let out a howl such as had never been heard in the underworld. The head bit and snapped. Hercules squeezed tighter. He lifted Cerberus high over his head and climbed up to daylight. Hercules was ferried back across the river Styz. All the while he kept a tight hold on Cerberus's necks.

In Mycenae, the people trembled to see Hercules carrying Hades's dog. Hercules went before the king and presented him with the beast. Eurystheus shrank back in fear. He screamed at Hercules to take the monster back to the underworld.

And so, the twelve labors of Hercules were completed. King Eurystheus was forced to admit that Hercules was a hero. He had done brave and mighty deeds. And he had rid the world of many beasts and monsters.

13. *Who guarded Geryon's cattle?*
14. *What was special about the apple trees of Hesperides?*
15. *How did Atlas try to trick Hercules?*

The Death of Hercules

Hercules went on to have many more adventures. And he married a beautiful woman named Deianira.

Now Deianira loved Hercules very much. But she sometimes doubted his love for her. One of Hercules's enemies gave Deianira what he said was a magic love potion. "Put it on Hercules's clothing. It will guarantee his love for you."

Deianira discovered too late that she had not been given a love potion. It was, in fact, poison from the tip of Hercules's own arrows. When she found this out, she'd already rubbed the liquid on Hercules's cloak. And she couldn't stop him in time from putting the cloak on.

The poison seeped into Hercules's skin. His body burned like fire. Even his great strength was no match for the poison. It killed him in moments.

The gods couldn't bear to see the earth's greatest hero in the dark underworld. Zeus came down in a chariot. He carried his son back to Mount Olympus to live with him there forever.

16. *What killed Hercules?*

17. *Why did Deianira want to give Hercules a love potion?*

18. *Where did Zeus take Hercules after he died?*

The Trojan War

Long ago, near the eastern end of the Mediterranean Sea, there was a great rich city. It was called Troy. Troy was destroyed many times. In this story, the Greeks explain how it fell one time.

The Judgment of Paris

The goddess of discord lived on Mount Olympus. Eris loved to cause arguments and unhappiness. Because of this, there were many places where she wasn't welcome.

Now the sea nymph Thetis was to be married to a king. All the goddesses but Eris were invited to the wedding. This made her very angry and more interested than ever in stirring things up.

Eris passed the wedding hall and tossed something in through the door. It was a golden apple marked "For the Fairest."

Of course, all the goddesses wanted the apple. They began arguing. At last the choice was narrowed down to three: Hera, Aphrodite, and Athena. Zeus refused to make the choice. He didn't want the goddesses angry with him.

"Go to Mount Ida, near Troy," Zeus told the three goddesses. "A handsome young man named Paris lives there. He is an excellent judge of beauty. Let him decide."

Paris was amazed when three beautiful goddesses appeared before him. Each wanted to win the strange beauty contest. Each offered Paris a bribe.

"Judge me the fairest," said Hera. "I will make you lord of all Europe and Asia!"

"Choose me," said Athena. "You will lead the Trojans to victory over the Greeks."

"Choose me, Paris," said Aphrodite. "And the fairest woman in the world shall be yours!"

Now Paris was not a very brave man. And he wasn't interested in power or wealth. But he did like women. So Paris gave Aphrodite the golden apple.

His decision was known as the Judgment of Paris. It led to the Trojan War, which lasted almost 10 years.

1. *Why did all the goddesses want the apple?*

2. *Why didn't Zeus want to choose the fairest goddess?*

3. *Why did Paris choose Aphrodite?*

The War

The fairest woman in the world was Helen. She was the daughter of Zeus and a mortal named Leda. Helen was so beautiful that every young man in Greece wanted to marry her. They came before her mother's mortal husband, a powerful king. Every man begged for her hand. The king was afraid that if he chose one man, the others would turn against him.

"Before I choose," he said to the anxious young men, "you must each make a promise. You must swear to support and protect me. You must also do this for the man I choose to be Helen's husband."

All the young men promised. The king chose Menelaus and made him king of Sparta.

Now Aphrodite still had to keep her promise to Paris. She knew Helen was the fairest woman in the world. And she knew exactly where to find her. Aphrodite led Paris to Sparta. Menelaus and Helen had married. They received Paris as their guest. They never thought his visit would cause any problems. Menelaus was a trusting man, and he soon left Sparta on a short journey. He left Paris alone with Helen.

Paris kidnapped Helen and carried her off to Troy. When Menelaus returned to Sparta, he discovered that his wife was gone. He called upon all of Greece to help him get back his queen. Young warriors from near and far answered the call. Remember, they had promised to support and protect the husband of Helen. An army gathered, and a thousand Greek ships sailed for Troy.

Nine years of battles followed. Many brave heroes died. The Greek army was strong, but the Trojan army was strong, too. The gods on Mount Olympus watched the fighting. They took sides and helped the different warriors.

By the end of the ninth year, the Greeks had surrounded the city. But they could not get inside it. Troy lay behind strong walls. The Trojans threw down rocks and spears at anyone who tried to climb them. It seemed the war would never end.

4. *Who was the fairest woman in the world? Who were her parents?*

5. *What started the battle?*

6. *How many Greek ships sailed for Troy?*

The Fall of Troy

The Greek general Odysseus finally came up with a plan. "We will pretend to give in," he said. "We'll go back to our ships, as if we were leaving. But we will have built a giant horse out of wood. The horse will be hollow. When the time comes, I will climb inside. So will you, and you, and you." Odysseus pointed to many of his best soldiers.

The Greeks built their wooden horse. On a moonless night, they pulled it to the walls of Troy. Then they boarded their ships and sailed out a short distance.

Next morning, the Trojan guards saw a strange sight. The sun shone on empty fields. There were no Greek tents and no Greek soldiers. Instead, a huge wooden horse stood before them.

"Hurrah!" one of the Trojan guards shouted. "The war is over. The Greeks have gone!"

Cries of joy swept through Troy. "The war is over! We have won!" The gates were thrown open. At last, the people could step outside the walls of their city.

"But what *is* this?" the Trojans asked as they walked around the horse. "What's it doing here? Where did it come from?"

"It's a trick!" one man shouted. "Beware the Greeks' gifts. I'm telling you, this is just one of their tricks!"

Upon hearing these words, many people drew back from the horse.

Entering Troy

Just then a group of Trojan soldiers came along. They were dragging a prisoner. "We found this Greek soldier hiding in the woods," they told Priam, the Trojan king. "We must put him to death. But first he shall answer some questions!"

"Don't kill me," the prisoner begged. "I am no friend of the Greeks. I ran away from their army. I wanted to join you. I'll tell you anything you want to know."

King Priam and the Trojans believed the prisoner. This was their mistake. He had really been sent by Odysseus and the Greeks.

"Tell us," said Priam, "about the great horse that stands before our gates."

"It was built by the Greeks. It is an offering to the goddess Athena. The horse is a powerful figure. It will protect anyone who owns it."

"Why, then," asked Priam, "did the Greeks leave it behind them?"

"It was too large and heavy to carry on their ships," the man answered. "They had no choice but to leave it."

When the people heard of the horse's power, they decided to bring it into Troy. Surely, it would protect the city forever. They put wheels under it and tied great straps to it. They pulled the wooden horse through their gates. Then the Trojans had a great feast. They ate and drank and celebrated the war's ending. They tired themselves out that night and fell into a deep sleep.

The Greeks in the wooden horse quietly swung open its hidden doors. They lowered ladders, climbed down, and ran back to the walls. They unlocked the gates.

Meanwhile, the Greek ships had returned to shore. The Greek soldiers poured through Troy's open gates. Six hours later, one of the world's proudest cities was a pile of ashes.

Aphrodite saved Helen from the fire and battle. Perhaps she was a bit sorry for the sorrow she'd caused. The war had started when Aphrodite led Paris to Helen and he carried her away to Troy. Aphrodite now led Helen to Menelaus. Her husband gladly took her back. Helen and Menelaus then returned with the Greek armies to Sparta.

7. *What was Odysseus's plan to win the war?*

8. *How did the Greeks convince the Trojans it wasn't a trick?*

9. *How did the Trojans get the giant horse into their city?*

Romulus and Remus

In their mythology, the Romans tried to explain the history of their nation. The story of Romulus and Remus describes the founding of the city of Rome. This myth uses the Roman names for the gods and the goddesses.

Youth

Two royal brothers lived in Italy. Their names were Amulius and Numitor. The older one, Numitor, became a king. He was a fair and gentle ruler. But Amulius was cruel and crafty. And he wanted to be king. He used force to steal the throne. Amulius and his soldiers drove Numitor out of his kingdom.

Numitor had two children, a son and a daughter. Amulius was afraid they might someday claim the throne. So Amulius had Numitor's son put to death. But he was afraid to kill Numitor's daughter, Silvia. He knew people would think him too cruel if he murdered an innocent girl.

Amulius came up with a plan. He made Silvia a priestess for the goddess Vesta. A priestess in the temple of Vesta was called a

Vestal. Vestals were not allowed to marry. Silvia would never have a son who could become king.

Silvia began her life in Vesta's temple. She tended the fire that honored the goddess of hearth and home. For a long time, it seemed that Amulius's plan was working. Silvia would never have a son to claim the throne.

But one day a handsome stranger came to the temple. He was strong and tall and had a fierce look in his eye. A lean gray wolf walked by the stranger's side. A woodpecker rode on his shoulder. When he saw the priestess, he fell in love with her. And Silvia could not help but return his love. For he was Mars, the great god of war.

Silvia and Mars had twin sons. Their names were Romulus and Remus. Amulius's plan had gone astray. At first he was frightened. Then he decided to act quickly to save his throne.

Amulius had Silvia thrown into prison for breaking her vows to Vesta. Then the king gave orders to get rid of Romulus and Remus. He had the babies placed in a basket and set adrift on the Tiber River. The cruel king knew the basket would fill with water and sink. The twins would drown.

But Amulius's plans failed again. The

Romulus and Remus

basket washed up on a bank of the river.
The babies were still alive. They lay there,
hungry and wailing.

In time a mother wolf came to the river
for a drink of water. Hearing the babies' cries,
she sniffed their basket. What were these
hairless shivering creatures?

Whatever they were, they needed help. The
wolf took the basket in her mouth and carried
Romulus and Remus back to her den. She
cared for them along with her own cubs. They
drank her milk. She taught them to wrestle
wolf-style. When they were older, she taught
them to hunt.

Romulus and Remus grew up as sons of
the wolf. They learned to be swift, bold, and
cunning. One day a shepherd discovered them

alone in the woods. The wolf-boys growled and showed their teeth, as any wolf cubs would. But the shepherd was a strong man. He grasped the boys firmly. He placed one under each arm and carried them toward his home. Romulus and Remus snarled and snapped. But they could not get away.

The mother wolf searched many days for her lost cubs. At last she gave up the search. Romulus and Remus had gone to a new home.

The shepherd brought the strange twins to his wife. "You have always wanted children," he said. "I think these two have been sent to us by the gods. I'm not sure if they're human. But whatever they are, they seem to be ours for the keeping."

The shepherd's wife reached out and gently patted each of the boys. They stopped growling and rubbed against her.

"Yes, we shall keep them," she said. "They will be our children."

The shepherd's wife taught Romulus and Remus to act like human beings. At first they didn't want to put on clothes or eat at a table. But in time they learned to talk and to walk upright. And they grew to love the shepherd and his wife.

The twins became expert shepherds themselves. They enjoyed tending their flocks.

Then, one fall day, a band of robbers attacked Remus. They stole the sheep and captured Remus. These robbers were from the kingdom of Amulius. They took Remus to the king's prison. Romulus heard what had happened and got ready to go after his brother.

"Wait," cried the man who had acted as his father. "Before you go, there are things you must know!"

1. *Who was the father of Romulus and Remus?*

2. *Who took care of the boys when they were little?*

3. *Which brother did the robbers take to prison?*

Royalty

The old shepherd told Romulus the incredible tale. "When you first learned to talk, both you and Remus said some strange things. You said you remembered floating in a basket. You spoke of a mother wolf who cared for you near the Tiber. As you spoke, I remembered a story I'd heard about King Amulius. It was said he had taken the throne from Numitor, his brother. He imprisoned Numitor's daughter and cast her twin babies into the Tiber River. It didn't take me long to realize that you and Remus were those twin babies. I found you near the Tiber."

Romulus was too surprised to speak. Suddenly he was no longer a simple peasant. Now he was the grandson of royalty. He was a prince.

"Go to your grandfather Numitor," the shepherd said. "He lives in a nearby land."

So Romulus set off. This was the first time Remus was not by his side. Romulus found Numitor and told him his story.

Numitor was silent for a time. He looked closely at Romulus. At last he spoke. "There is no doubt about it," he said. "You have your mother's eyes, and you carry yourself like a prince. Your story rings true. You are my grandson. And you say your brother is a prisoner of Amulius?"

"Yes," said Romulus. "And I will free him. Then we'll get you your throne back."

"But how will you do this?" Numitor asked.

"I have many friends," said Romulus. "I will call on the other shepherds for help. With sticks and stones and whatever weapons we can find, we will fight Amulius."

Romulus was the son of Mars, the god of war. He put together a fierce army. He turned a band of shepherds and some servants of Numitor's into skillful soldiers. They marched on Amulius's kingdom.

The fighting lasted only an hour. Romulus was too smart for the king. He rescued his brother Remus. Together they broke into Amulius's throne room. There they found the king, hiding and shaking as his kingdom fell. Romulus and Remus killed Amulius and declared Numitor the rightful king.

For some time, Romulus and Remus sat by their grandfather's side in the royal court. But the young men often thought of their days in the woods. The spirit of the wolf still lived inside them. They decided that they would have to leave the kingdom.

"We will found a new city," they said. "We will build it by the Tiber River, where the mother wolf saved our lives."

And so Romulus and Remus left Numitor. With a loyal band of men, they went to the banks of the Tiber.

"We will build the city over there!" cried Remus.

"No," said Romulus. "The correct spot is right where we're standing!"

For the first time, the brothers quarreled. They argued violently. Some of the men took Romulus's side. Others sided with Remus.

At last the brothers called upon the gods. They would let Jupiter, Juno, and the other great gods choose the site. The gods decided in favor of Romulus. He and his men began at once. They marked out the boundaries of the new city. But Remus was jealous. He got angry. Remus knocked down the markers as quickly as Romulus set them. Fighting broke out. In the battle, Remus was killed.

Romulus fell to his knees and wailed when he saw his brother lying dead. But he could not bring him back.

When he stopped crying, he told his men, "We've come here to build. We must begin."

They built a fine proud city on seven hills. Its first king was Romulus. The city was named after him. It was called Rome.

"One day Rome will be the greatest city in the world," Romulus declared.

Until the day he died, Romulus kept an empty throne beside his own. He did it to show that his brother shared his power.

4. *How did the brothers find out they were really royalty?*

5. *Why was Romulus good at putting an army together?*

6. *What did he build?*

Pronunciation Guide

> *Every effort has been made to present native pronunciations of the unusual names in this book. Sometimes experts differed in their opinions, however, or no pronunciation could be found. Also, certain foreign-language sounds were felt to be unpronounceable by today's readers. In these cases, editorial license was exercised in selecting pronunciations.*

Key

Capital letters are used to represent stressed syllables. For example, the word *ugly* would be written here as "UHG lee."

The letter or letters used to show pronunciation have the following sounds:

a   as in *map* and *glad*
ah as in *pot* and *cart*
aw as in *fall* and *lost*
ch as in *chair* and *child*
e   as in *let* and *care*
ee as in *feet* and *please*
ey as in *play* and *face*
g   as in *gold* and *girl*

hy as in *huge* and *humor*
i as in *my* and *high*
ih as in *sit* and *clear*
j as in *jelly* and *gentle*
k as in *skill* and *can*
ky as in *cute*
l as in *long* and *pull*
my as in *mule*
ng as in *sing* and *long*
o as in *slow* and *go*
oo as in *cool* and *move*
ow as in *cow* and *round*
s as in *soon* and *cent*
sh as in *shoe* and *sugar*
th as in *thin* and *myth*
u as in *put* and *look*
uh as in *run* and *up*
y as in *you* and *yesterday*
z as in *zoo* and *pairs*

Guide

Aeetes: ee EE teez

Aegeus: EE juhs

Aethra: EE thruh

Amazons: AM uh zahnz

Amulius: uh MYOO lee uhs

Aphrodite: af ro DI tee

Apollo: uh PAHL o

Arachne: uh RAK nee

Ares: ER eez

Argonauts: AHR go nahts

Argus: AHR guhs

Argo: AHR go

Ariadne: er ee AD nee

Artemis: AHR tuh mihs

Athena: uh THEE nuh

Bacchus: BAK uhs

Centaur: SEN tahr

Ceres: SEE reez

Chiron: KI ruhn

Colchis: KOL kihs

Crete: KREET

Cronus: KRO nuhs

Cyclopes: SI klo peesz

Cyclops: SI klahps

Daedalus: DED uh luhs

Danae: DAN uh ee

Deianira: dee yuh NIH ruh

Demeter: dih MEE tur

Diana: di AN ah

Dictys: DIHK tihs

Dionysus: di uh NI suhs

Echo: EK o

Epimetheus: e pih MEE thee uhs

Eris: ER ihs

Eurystheus: yuh RIHS thee uhs

Galatea: gal uh TEE uh

Geryon: JER ee uhn

Gorgons: GOR guhnz

Hades: HEY deez

Helen: HEL uhn

Hephaestus: hih FES tuhs

Hera: HEER uh

Heracles: HER uh kleez

Hercules: HER kyoo leez

Hermes: HUR meez

Hesperides: hes PER ih deez

Hippolyta: hih PAHL ih tuh

Hydra: HI druh

Icarus: IHK ur ruhs

Ida: I duh

Iolaus: i uh LEY uhs

Jason: JEY suhn

Juno: JOO no

Jupiter: JOO pih tur

Leda: LEE duh

Mars: MAHRZ

Medea: mih DEE uh

Medusa: muh DOO suh

Menelaus: men uh LEY uhs

Mercury: MUR kyur ee

Midas: MI duhs

Minerva: mih NUR vuh

Minos: MI nuhs

Minotaur: MIHN uh tahr

Mount Olympus: o LIHM puhs

Mycenae: mi SEE nee

Narcissus: nahr SIHS uhs

Nemea: nih MEE uh

Neptune: NEP toon

Numitor: NOO mih tor

Odysseus: o DIHS ee uhs

Pactolus River: pak TO luhs

Pan: PAN

Pandora: pan DOR uh

Paris: PER ihs

Pelias: PEE lee uhs

Persephone: pur SEF uh nee

Perseus: PUR see uhs

Phineas: FIHN ee uhs

Pluto: PLOO to

Polydectes: pahl ih DEK teez

Poseidon: po SI duhn

Priam: PRI uhm

Prometheus: pro MEE thee uhs

Pygmalion: pihg MEYL yuhn

Pyramus: PIHR u muhs

Remus: REE muhs

Rhea: REE uh

Romulus: RAHM yuh luhs

Silvia: SIHL vee uh

Sparta: SPAHR tuh

Stymphalus Lake: stihm FEY luhs

Theseus: THEE see uhs

Thessaly: THES uh lee

Thisbe: THIHZ bee

Thrace: THREYS

Tiber: TI bur

Titans: TI tuhnz

Tmolus: TIHM o luhs

Trojan: TRO juhn

Troy: TROY

Venus: VEE nuhs

Vesta: VES tuh

Vulcan: VUHL kuhn

Zeus: ZOOS

DATE DUE			

DOCTOR WHO

BBC CHILDREN'S BOOKS

UK | USA | Canada | Ireland | Australia
India | New Zealand | South Africa

BBC Children's Books are published by Puffin Books,
part of the Penguin Random House group of companies
whose addresses can be found at global.penguinrandomhouse.com.

puffinbooks.com

Penguin
Random House
UK

First published by Puffin Books 2011
This edition first published by Puffin Books 2015

001

Written by Trevor Baxendale
Copyright © BBC Worldwide Limited, 2015

BBC, DOCTOR WHO (word marks, logos and devices),
TARDIS, DALEKS, CYBERMAN and K-9 (word marks and devices) are
trademarks of the British Broadcasting Corporation and are used under licence.
BBC logo © BBC, 1996. Doctor Who logo © BBC, 2009

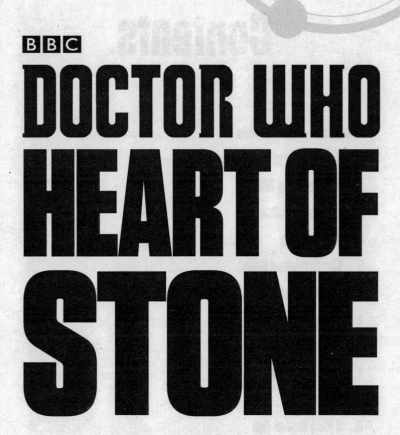

BBC

DOCTOR WHO
HEART OF
STONE

Trevor Baxendale

PUFFIN

Contents

Prologue
Night Terrors

Ralph Conway woke up in the middle of the night. He could hear dogs barking outside.

Ralph climbed out of bed with a groan. He wasn't so young anymore, and he was stiff as a board.

The dogs were barking furiously now.

Ralph looked out of the window, but it was difficult to see anything in the dark. Something was driving those dogs wild, though.

'Four o'clock in the morning!' Ralph grumbled, as he pulled a coat on over his pyjamas.

He went downstairs and switched on the kitchen light. He hoped it would scare off any intruders. Then he pulled on a pair of boots and unlocked the back door. He paused to pick up a torch and a heavy walking stick. Anyone caught lurking outside would get a whack with that stick!

It was a chilly, moonlit night. The dogs had stopped barking now, which Ralph thought was strange. The sudden silence was frightening.

Ralph walked slowly across the yard. The dogs were hanging back, whining, almost as if they were scared. That didn't make Ralph feel any better. He had lived on the farm all his life and he knew the area well – it was isolated and exposed.

Suddenly there was a terrific noise – a great, splintering crash in the night, like a juggernaut plowing through a wall at top speed.

The dogs ran yelping back to the farmhouse.Ralph, his heart pounding, shone his torch into the darkness. The wall at the end of the yard was completely destroyed – there was rubble everywhere. Something huge and heavy had smashed clean through.

Ralph moved cautiously forward, stick raised. He would defend himself if he had to.

But no matter where Ralph shone his torch, he saw nothing other than shadows. Apart from the damaged wall, there was nothing to see. There were lumps of stone strewn all around the yard, though, where the wall had been hit.

Through the break in the wall, Ralph could see a car in the distance. The glow of its headlights moved along the main road on the far side of the valley. It was too far away for him to hear it, but it made him think. It was possible, Ralph thought, that a lorry could have crashed into the wall. The bend in the road going past the farm was a well-known accident black spot. A reckless driver could easily lose control of his vehicle.

But where was it now? There was no sign of any car or lorry at all. And Ralph hadn't even heard an engine.

But there was *something*.

The noise of stone moving across stone – a dull, heavy scrape.

Ralph swung his torchlight around the yard, but there was nothing to see. The barn, the tractor, a rusty old plough. Clumps of straw and mud and some puddles reflecting the light of the moon.

Scrape, scrape . . .

There *was* something there, Ralph was sure of it. Something moving in the shadows. He aimed the torch again, and this time his hand was trembling. The light flickered across a coil of hosepipe; the water trough; a collection of tools leaning against the outhouse . . .

And then he saw it.

Something huge – lumbering – walking on two legs like some kind of giant . . .

And then it was gone, disappearing into the

shadows again.

Ralph's heart hammered in his chest and his mouth went dry. He shone the torch around the yard, but there was no sign of the strange figure.

Whatever it was . . . had gone.

Ralph licked his lips. Perhaps it had just been his imagination. That was the only explanation, surely. He was still half asleep. His mind was playing tricks on him.

The dogs were whimpering again. Ralph peered down at the rocks strewn across the yard.

They shone like bone in the cold moonlight and Ralph shivered.

Chapter 1

Conway Farm

The TARDIS appeared in the middle of a pigsty. Startled, the pigs ran around in panic, snorting and squealing and slipping in the wet straw.

Eventually the harsh wheezing of its engines diminished and the TARDIS stood, proud and blue, next to the water trough.

The Doctor stepped out of the TARDIS and immediately greeted the pigs. 'Good morning!'

But the pigs had already decided to ignore the box and anyone who emerged from inside it. As long as they were fed and watered, they didn't really mind who shared their sty.

The Doctor looked like a tall young man with a shock of untidy dark hair and mischievous, deep-set eyes. He wore a tweed jacket and bow tie, with narrow trousers tucked into old boots. He smiled at the pigs as they snuffled around in the straw. 'Lovely morning!'

'Pigs!' said Amy Pond, as she followed the Doctor out of the TARDIS. She wrinkled her nose. 'Phew . . .'

'*That* is the scent of the countryside,' said Rory Williams, as he stepped out into the manure covering the ground. 'Yuck.'

Amy and Rory were the Doctor's current travelling companions. She was young, pretty, with striking red hair and trendy clothes. He was tall, rather awkward and dressed in jeans and a warm padded jacket.

Not in the least bit put off by the pigs, the Doctor locked the TARDIS, clearly intending to stay. 'Just what we need,' he told his friends. 'A nice breath of fresh country air.'

'Fresh?' Amy repeated doubtfully.

'Hey!' a voice called out. 'You can't leave that thing in there like that!'

They all turned to see a young woman striding towards the pigsty in mud-splattered wellies and a thick, padded coat. She had dark hair tied back and a seriously cross look on her face.

The three travellers turned as one to look at the TARDIS. The space and time machine was disguised as an old police box and so it looked decidedly out of place in the pigsty. But then, the TARDIS looked a bit out of place *anywhere*.

'You'll frighten Old Percy,' the young woman told them. 'She's pregnant, y'know!'

'Percy?' said Rory with a frown.

'Pregnant?' said Amy.

'Long story,' sighed the woman. 'Look, you can't stay in there. You'll have to leave the box where it is, I suppose.'

The Doctor, Amy and Rory climbed over the low fence surrounding the pen and introduced themselves.

'My name's Jess,' the woman said. 'I've come to feed Old Percy. She needs twice as much as normal – she's eating for six at least.'

Jess heaved a bucket of slops into the trough and the pigs got stuck in, heads down and ears flopping. The yard was quickly filled with the sound of chomping and snorting.

'How on Earth did you get that thing in there anyway?' Jess asked, nodding at the TARDIS.

'Well, it just sort of materialised there,' replied the Doctor.

Jess raised an eyebrow. 'Oh, it did, did it?'

'Ask Old Percy.'

Jess patted the sow's back. 'She's a bit busy now,' she said with a smile. 'I'll ask her later.'

'Do you work here, then?' Amy asked.

'Of course. This is Conway Farm. It may not look

like much, but I call it home.'

The little farm overlooked a wide valley. The sky above was full of clouds and the promise of rain. A sharp breeze carried the smell of grass and soil and animals across the fields, and Amy shivered in her short skirt. She wasn't dressed for farming.

'Let's get you in for a cup of tea,' laughed Jess. 'We don't often get visitors here!'

They followed Jess along a narrow, rutted track until they reached the farmhouse. A burly man with a hard, grizzled face was busy repairing a broken wall. He wore thick gloves to protect his hands and an old flat cap.

Rory whistled when he saw the full extent of the damage. There was rubble and bits of broken brick scattered everywhere. 'What happened here?' he asked.

'Somethin' costin' me time an' money,' growled the man. He didn't sound at all happy.

'This is my dad, Ralph Conway,' said Jess. She introduced the Doctor, Amy and Rory.

'How do,' grunted Ralph, touching his cap before returning to his work.

'There was an accident here last night,' explained Jess. 'Smashed the wall to bits. Dad's got to fix it.'

'An accident?' repeated the Doctor. He was looking

14

at the smashed stones all over the yard.

'We think a lorry or something must have crashed into it last night,' Jess continued. 'Plenty of trucks miss the bend in the road and skid if they're not careful.'

The Doctor looked at the road and nodded thoughtfully. 'Yes, I see. Or rather, I don't.'

'I beg your pardon?' Jess said.

'No skid marks,' said the Doctor. 'Nothing to show any kind of vehicle coming off the road.'

'Uh oh,' said Rory quietly to Amy. 'He's getting all curious . . .'

Amy smiled. 'Probably thinks it was hit by a meteorite or something.'

The Doctor had picked up a piece of stone from the ground. It was a pale grey colour, roughly the size of a tennis ball. He weighed it in his hand and sniffed it. Then he looked around. There were plenty of stones like this littered across the yard.

'All this damage,' said the Doctor. 'And no sign of a lorry or a car, or anything.'

Ralph was watching the Doctor carefully. It was clear that he was interested in what the Doctor had to say. He straightened up and said, 'Well, what do you think did it? Cos I can't work it out!'

The Doctor was smiling. 'I've really no idea,' he said. 'But I'd love to find out!'

'Are you from the insurance company?' asked Jess, as if suddenly struck by a thought. 'Come to assess the damage?'

'No, I'm just a nosy parker,' the Doctor replied. 'For instance, this stone interests me enormously.' He held up the fragment of grey rock between his finger and thumb for all to see. 'This isn't local stone, is it?'

'No,' answered Ralph. 'There's loads of it around this morning, though. I thought it might have fallen off the back of the lorry.'

'The lorry that doesn't actually exist,' pointed out Amy.

Ralph shrugged. 'I dunno. But it isn't stone from around here – that much I do know. I thought maybe it had come from Derbyshire.'

'It's from considerably further away than Derbyshire, Mr Conway,' said the Doctor. He held the stone up towards the sky. 'This piece of rock has come all the way from the moon!'

Chapter 2

A Hole in the Wall

The Doctor was sitting at the kitchen table, examining the lump of grey rock with his sonic screwdriver.

Amy and Rory were holding mugs of hot tea, while Jess opened a packet of chocolate biscuits and put them on the table.

'Got any Jammie Dodgers?' asked the Doctor without looking up. 'Always liked a Jammie Dodger.'

'Sorry, just these,' smiled Jess.

'These are fine,' said Rory, delving into the packet.

'You'd best take them away,' Amy told Jess, 'before the Cookie Monster here eats them all.'

The Doctor looked up sharply. 'Did someone say monster?'

'Not that kind of monster, silly,' laughed Amy.

'Anyway – it's breakfast,' Rory protested, munching on another biscuit.

'Breakfast?' queried Jess. She was peering into the oven, where a large pot was simmering. 'It's nearly time for dinner.'

'It's hard to keep track of time where we come from,' explained Amy. 'That smells good, though. What's cooking?'

'Lamb stew,' smiled Jess. 'Don't worry, there's enough for everyone.'

'Oh, no, we're not staying –' Amy said, but the Doctor interrupted her with a loud exclamation.

'Look at this!' The Doctor shut down his sonic screwdriver with a satisfied click. 'Definitely moon rock,' he announced. 'High concentrations of anorthite, pyroxene, mare basalts and titanium. And lots of armalcolite – a new and unique mineral named after the crew of Apollo 11: *Arm*strong, *Al*drin and *Col*lins. So – without a doubt, moon rock.'

'But how can that be?' asked Rory, reaching for another chocolate digestive. 'I mean, all the way here from the moon . . . ?'

'Did it come down in a meteorite or something?' wondered Amy.

'Meteorite?' queried Jess.

'Yeah, you know . . .' said the Doctor, sitting back and folding his arms. His gaze never left the moon rock, however. 'Lumps of iron, rock, bits and pieces

18

and what-have-you, flying through space and falling into Earth's gravitational pull.'

'So you mean it could be a chunk of the moon that's actually fallen to Earth?'

The Doctor pursed his lips. 'Doubt it. Most meteors burn up in Earth's atmosphere. Very few reach the ground – and if they do, then they're big enough to cause a heck of a lot of damage.'

'There *is* a lot of damage,' Jess pointed out.

The Doctor was still staring at the rock. 'If a meteorite this big had survived the trip through the atmosphere and landed in your front yard, then the whole farm would have been flattened.'

'Oh. I see.'

'There has to be another explanation.'

'Such as?' asked Amy.

The Doctor didn't reply. Instead, he simply picked up the moon rock and dashed out of the kitchen.

When the others caught up, he was standing in the middle of the yard holding his sonic screwdriver aloft. The tip glowed green as he waved it about.

'What is that thing?' wondered Jess.

'Sonic screwdriver,' explained Rory, trying to sound like an expert. 'But it does a lot more than just . . . driving screws.'

The Doctor wheeled around the yard with the

sonic, pausing occasionally to check the readings. Eventually he shoved it back into his jacket pocket and harrumphed. 'No sign of any alien spacecraft technology, teleport beam or quantum link. It's a complete mystery.' He sounded insulted, as if nothing had any right to be a complete mystery to him.

'Well something must have brought it here,' insisted Amy.

The Doctor tossed the moon rock from hand to hand, wondering. Then he wandered over to where Ralph Conway was still working on the wall. 'How's it going, Mr Conway?'

Ralph straightened up, wincing slightly and holding his back. 'Just about done,' he rumbled. 'It'll have to do for now, at least.'

The Doctor surveyed the repair work. You could see quite easily where the moon rocks had been used to fill in the hole, but it was a remarkably good job, nonetheless. 'You've had to use a lot of moon stone,' the Doctor observed. 'And yet it all seems to fit together quite nicely.'

'Well, that's the strangest thing,' agreed Ralph. 'I've no idea what happened to the rest of the wall, but those rocks you say come from the moon seemed to do the trick all right. It's a case of having to make do and mend, Doctor.'

'You've missed a bit,' noted Rory, joining them. He pointed to a hole the size of his fist on the top edge of the wall.

'No, he hasn't,' said the Doctor. He darted forward and placed the moon rock he still had in his hand in the space. It fitted perfectly.

'Well, I'll be . . .' Ralph Conway took off his cap and scratched his head.

'That was lucky,' laughed Rory.

'Nothing to do with luck, Rory.' The Doctor was pacing up and down the wall, rubbing his fingers together as he inspected the wall. 'Dry stone wall, remember. Every piece has a place. These moon rocks are all the exact size and shape necessary to repair the wall.'

Rory frowned. 'But that's impossible – isn't it?'

The Doctor looked up at him, his eyes gleaming. 'No more impossible than finding chunks of the moon on this farm in the first place.'

Chapter 3

The First Visitor

The Doctor was examining the area all around the wall, front and back, when a sleek red sports car pulled in through the gates and stopped in the middle of the yard with a cheery growl of its exhaust.

Jess walked over to the car, a look of pure delight on her face.

The driver climbed nimbly out of the car, equally happy. He was tall, smooth-faced and good-looking. He wore wire-framed glasses and was dressed in clean corduroy trousers and a fashionable sports jacket. 'Hi there, sweetheart,' he said, embracing Jess warmly.

'Who's the lucky fella?' asked Amy.

Jess led the man over. 'This is Chris,' she said, introducing Amy and Rory. 'My fiancé.'

'Hey – Amy and I were engaged once,' said Rory with a smile. 'We're married now, though. Mr and Mrs Pond!'

'Great to meet you,' said Chris, shaking hands. 'I hope I'm not intruding on anything?'

'No, we're just passing through,' Amy assured him.

'But they're staying for dinner with us,' Jess said. 'I insist. There's plenty for everyone!'

Chris was still smiling broadly, but Amy thought she could detect a slight frown above his eyes. It was almost as if there was something on his mind that he wanted to tell Jess, but would have to keep to himself for now.

'That's great,' Chris was saying. 'The more the merrier.'

'Dinner will be ready in about twenty minutes,' Jess told them. 'Time for Dad to get cleaned up at least.'

Ralph Conway was standing by the wall with the Doctor. They were both examining a rock in minute detail, the Doctor's fingers wiggling over it as he talked about the geology of the moon. When he heard Jess call him, Ralph looked up. He nodded at Chris, but there was no smile. Chris waved back and then followed Jess into the farmhouse with Rory and Amy.

'Trouble?' wondered the Doctor. He had noticed the way Ralph's lips had tightened in disapproval when his daughter's fiancé had arrived.

'Who knows?' Ralph replied.

The Doctor shrugged. 'None of my business, but

I can't help noticing that you don't seem too happy to see that young lad.'

Ralph raised an eyebrow, amused by the Doctor's description of Chris as a young lad. The Doctor didn't look any older than Chris himself. 'You're right . . .' Ralph grumbled. 'It isn't any of your business.'

'But you don't approve of him?'

'Jess is my only daughter. I don't want her hurt.'

'You think that might happen?'

Ralph sighed heavily. 'Chris Jenkins is not from around here, Doctor. He's all right in himself – but he's not a country man, if you know what I mean.'

'Ah,' said the Doctor. 'A townie?'

'He doesn't understand farming. And that's all Jess has ever known.'

'She's young. She'll learn.'

'That's what worries me.'

Chapter 4
Dinner Time

Dinner was a lively affair, with an excellent lamb
stew served with new potatoes garnished with mint.
Everyone agreed that Jess had done an excellent job.
Even Ralph Conway looked content. If he disapproved
of Jess's boyfriend, then he made every effort not to
show it during the meal.

They talked about the weather and the farm and
Percy the pregnant pig. But the conversation turned
eventually, and naturally, to the disturbance of the
previous night, the broken wall and, of course, the
strange appearance of the moon rocks.

Chris Jenkins was doubtful. 'Moon rock? I
mean, *really*?'

'That's what the Doctor says,' Amy replied, sipping
her coffee. She held the mug cupped in both hands for
warmth. Rory's arm was around her shoulder.

Chris looked at the Doctor. 'Are you qualified to make that pronouncement?'

'Oh, yes,' the Doctor said. 'Extremely very qualified. And the sonic screwdriver never lies.'

'But the whole idea is absurd,' Chris insisted.

'Are *you* qualified to make that pronouncement?'

'As a matter of fact, I am,' Chris replied evenly. 'I'm a research technician at Henson Labs. I specialise in geochemistry and I've made quite a study of moon rock.'

'You never told me that,' said Jess.

Chris shrugged. 'You know I don't like to talk about my work too much. But the *Apollo* space missions brought back over 380kg of rock samples from the moon landings in the 1970s.'

'Wow,' said Rory. 'And you've seen them?'

'We were lent some samples once. I had to make a study of the cosmic ray and radiation history of the mineral content.' Chris's face broke into a smile. 'It was pretty boring, to be honest. But I have actually handled moon rock, and not many people can say that.'

'That's true,' said the Doctor.

'We could only touch them using gloves and special tools, though,' Chris continued. 'And the security was amazing. Did you know that moon rock is one of the most valuable substances on the planet?'

'Because it's so rare, I expect,' said Jess.

'Not so rare anymore,' said Amy drily.

'NASA still holds most of the samples,' Chris said. 'But many pieces were given away as presents by the US government to foreign countries. Moon rock is rarer than diamonds. Sometimes pieces are sold illegally on the black market at hugely inflated prices – but more often than not they're fakes.'

'How long ago was this?' asked the Doctor. 'When you worked on the moon samples, I mean.'

'Erm – a few years ago. We're currently studying the effects of UV light on lava and ash samples from the Eyjafjallajökull volcano in Iceland.'

'You should check some of the moon samples we have here,' suggested Rory. 'Could be useful.'

Chris shook his head. 'I don't think so. For one thing, I can't give permission to use the lab facilities. And anyway, I doubt very much that it *is* actual moon rock out there.'

'Well, it is,' the Doctor said.

Chris shook his head, clearly reaching the conclusion that the Doctor was talking rubbish. 'It's nonsense, really.'

'Is it possible there could be a mistake?' wondered Jess, trying to balance both sides of the argument. 'You've got to admit, Doctor, that there's no logical reason for lumps of the moon to be scattered around our farm.'

'I'd like to run some more tests on the rocks,' the Doctor admitted. 'I might know more then.'

'Sorry I can't help,' said Chris. 'I mean, even if I was allowed, I couldn't do it. We're mad busy at the lab with the volcanic ash. Worked off our feet.'

'Not hard work, though, is it?' said Ralph Conway. He had been quiet for most of the meal, preferring to concentrate on eating instead of talking. He had been brought up in a strict family, where no one was even allowed to speak during meal times.

'Oh, Dad . . .' Jess started. 'Just because it's not farm work . . .'

'No, it's OK,' said Chris. 'I understand. I don't do much physical work in my job. It's all up here.' He tapped his forehead. 'But I do keep myself fit. I go to the gym three times a week.'

'Hmm,' said Ralph, wiping his lips on a napkin. He clearly wasn't impressed. He got up from the table and excused himself, preferring not to go to bed too late. 'Farm chores start early,' he grumbled.

'Do you think there might be any more disturbances during the night?' asked Jess. 'Meteorites or crashing lorries or whatever?'

'I doubt it!' laughed Chris.

The Doctor stood up and looked directly at Chris. 'I'm positively counting on it.'

Chapter 5
The Uninvited Guest

The Doctor stepped outside and drew a deep breath.
It was cold and dark. He looked up at the night sky,
searching out familiar stars and constellations through
the gaps in the clouds.

It always paid to check that everything was as it
should be.

The moon glowed softly.

The Doctor frowned slightly. How could bits of
the moon suddenly end up all the way down here, on
Earth? And how could they match the size and shape
of the stones in Ralph Conway's wall? And why was
Chris Jenkins so touchy about the whole subject of
moon rock?

The Doctor's lips twitched into a smile. He loved a good mystery.

He retrieved the stone from the wall where he had placed it earlier and set off towards the TARDIS. He had instruments on-board that could tell him a lot more about the origin and structure of the moon rock in his hand.

As he walked up the hill towards the pigsty, a dark cloud drifted across the face of the moon and plunged the farm into an eerie darkness. It may only have been the Doctor's imagination, but it seemed to grow suddenly colder.

And there was a strange feeling in the air, a kind of tension, like the calm just before a storm broke.

The TARDIS windows were shining brightly in the darkness, and the Doctor hurried on.

In the farmhouse kitchen, Amy was helping Jess clear the dirty plates from the table, while Rory and Chris loaded them into the dishwasher.

'So, how did you two meet?' Rory asked. He liked Chris. He seemed decent, if a little overconfident, but Rory didn't mind that.

'Market day,' Chris replied. He smiled at Jess. 'Our eyes met across a herd of cows, and it was love at first sight.'

'Yeah, right,' said Jess ruefully. She scraped some leftovers into a recycling bucket. The pigs would get that later. 'As I remember, Chris stood in a fresh cow pat and blamed me for it.'

Amy laughed. 'Blamed you?'

'It came from one of her cows,' argued Chris.

Jess sighed. It was clearly a well-worn story. 'He was in a suit, with brand-new shoes. I helped clean him up. Things just went on from there.'

'So, I suppose I've got plenty to thank the silly cow for,' Chris said, and they both laughed.

With the dishwasher fully loaded, Jess made a fresh lot of coffee and asked Rory how he had met Amy.

'Oh, we knew each other from when we were kids,' he said, slightly embarrassed.

'Oh!' Jess seemed delighted. 'Childhood sweethearts. And what about the Doctor? Where does he fit in?'

'Erm, the same, really. Amy's known him since she was seven. Sort of.'

'Oh . . . ' Jess looked a little confused. 'Well, he's quite a character. Odd, but in a nice way.'

'I'll be sure to tell him that,' promised Amy with a smile. She picked up her jacket. 'I'm going up to the TARDIS to see how he's getting on.'

Rory made to follow, but she shook her head. 'No, you stay here. Enjoy your coffee. Back soon. See ya!'

Amy shivered as she stepped outside. It was cosy and warm in the farmhouse, but out here it was certainly getting chilly.

She folded her arms tightly and hurried across the yard, heading for the TARDIS. She could see the roof lamp and windows from here, shining out through the night. The sight always gave her a tingle of excitement.

She wondered what the Doctor was up to. She could just imagine him tinkering with the TARDIS control console, fussing around it from panel to panel, checking read-outs and gauges, utterly engrossed in some kind of scientific experiment.

Well, enough of all that, thought Amy. The Doctor could come back and spend some time with ordinary folk, enjoy a cup of coffee, proper conversation. Worry about the moon rocks in the morning.

Amy stepped past the water trough and headed up the slope – just as something huge and powerful suddenly rose up in front of her, right out of the darkness. It filled her vision like a wall of grey stone.

Amy opened her mouth to cry out, but it was too late. The great lump of rock bore down on her like a hammer on an anvil.

Chapter 6

Rock Monster

Amy was paralysed with fear for a second. The huge grey figure loomed over her like a statue – but a statue that could move. It was easily two-and-a-half metres tall, and looked as if it had been hewn from a solid lump of granite.

The creature reached towards her and–

The Doctor grabbed Amy and hauled her quickly out of the way.

The rock creature made an angry noise that sounded like a pile of house bricks being dragged across concrete. It turned, slowly but heavily, a pair of dark holes in its lumpy face serving as eyes.

Its hollow stare centred on its prey and it growled again.

'What is it?' Amy gasped.

'No idea,' replied the Doctor. 'Saw it on the

TARDIS monitor. Look out!'

The creature lashed out heavily. One rock-like fist crashed into a water trough, denting the steel and sending a spray of icy water into the night.

The Doctor and Amy backed away, heading for the farmhouse, just as Jess and Rory came out of it, eyes widening in horror as they saw the creature.

Chris appeared in the kitchen window, a look of shock and terror on his face. In less than a second, he had turned and run into the next room.

'Back inside!' ordered the Doctor, rushing straight past Jess and Rory.

Amy followed the Doctor, yelling, 'Right behind you!'

Rory was about to turn and pelt after them, but a scream from Jess made him pause. The rock monster swung a massive arm, missing Jess by centimetres, but caving in the side of the Land Rover parked outside the house. The door buckled and glass exploded across the yard.

Rory picked up a spare shovel, checked its weight in his hands, and then swung it like a cricket bat at the monster. The shovel connected with a resounding *clang!* and Rory felt the vibration running up his arms and into his shoulders like an electric shock.

The rock monster turned its attention from Jess to Rory with a gravelly snarl. Rory stared up at the creature. The shovel, which was still quivering like a tuning fork in his numbed fingers, slipped from his grasp.

The monster advanced slowly and purposefully towards Rory.

And then Jess was pulling him back into the farmhouse and slamming the door behind them. She scrabbled for the bolts at the top and bottom.

'That won't stop it,' said the Doctor.

And even as he spoke, the kitchen door shuddered with the impact of a giant stone fist.

'Quick, barricade it!' said Amy, trying to push the heavy kitchen table across the door. The others joined in, heaving the table into place, the coffee mugs rolling around and smashing on the floor.

But the creature wouldn't be put off so easily.

A second fist burst through the remains of the door. The big table skidded backwards, flung aside like an old cardboard box.

A third and final assault on the door reduced it to matchwood.

Chapter 7

Run or Fight

Shards of wood hurtled around the kitchen as the rock monster smashed its way in. The table was crushed, dashed aside, and then the whole room seemed to shake as the creature forced its way inside. The door frame tore loose from the surrounding brickwork, caught on the stone giant's bulky shoulders.

Ralph Conway's dogs were going berserk. Neither could understand what was happening, but both knew an intruder when they saw one. They snapped and barked and bared their fangs, jumping up at the creature as it seemed to fill the room.

The terrible racket had already brought Ralph running downstairs. 'What in the blue blazes is going on?' he thundered.

But Ralph could immediately see the danger his dogs were in. They could bark as much as they liked, but the thing that had forced its way into his house was just too powerful.

So Ralph grabbed both dogs by the collar and hauled them out of the kitchen, still yelping and barking.

The Doctor and Rory were trying to slow the monster down, throwing kitchen chairs, pots and pans and anything else they could lay their hands on at it. They finally gave up when an orange, hurled in desperation by Rory, bounced harmlessly off the creature's head.

'An orange?' the Doctor spluttered at Rory.

'Nothing left to chuck,' said Rory hopelessly.

'Time to go,' the Doctor said. They backed out of the kitchen, into the narrow passageway that connected the back of the house to the front. The rock monster growled menacingly, crunching its way across the stone floor of the kitchen in pursuit.

Ralph was struggling with the dogs. One broke free, snapping its jaws at anything that moved. It dived past the Doctor, heading for the kitchen. Ralph lunged after it, yelling for it to come back.

But it was too late. The dog snarled at the rock monster, but one savage swipe of its arm sent the hound spinning across the room.

'Get back!' shouted the Doctor, grabbing Ralph by the arm. But the farmer tore free, cursing the monster with every breath.

Then the creature reached out, grasped Ralph Conway in one giant, crag-like hand and hurled him backwards.

Ralph landed heavily in the passageway, completely stunned. The Doctor and Rory dragged him into the front room, where Jess and Amy were waiting with Chris Jenkins.

Chris had been cowering in the front room ever since he had seen the creature through the kitchen window. His face was white with fear, but he knew he had to do something now. He just didn't know what.

'Close the door!' screamed Jess.

Chris jumped up and slammed the door shut – but it was a useless gesture. Within seconds, the entire wall was disintegrating in a cloud of plaster dust as the rock creature forced its way through.

'It's unstoppable,' gasped Chris. He sounded utterly panic-stricken.

The rock creature stepped into the front room with a slow, ominous scraping sound. It surveyed the five people carefully, its blank eye sockets full of darkness.

'What is it, Doctor?' asked Rory fearfully.

'More importantly – what does it *want*?' wondered the Doctor.

'What does that matter?' asked Chris. He ran from one side of the room to another in panic. 'It's going to kill us all if we don't do something fast!'

'I'm open to suggestions,' said the Doctor.

'Well, here's mine,' replied Chris. 'Run for it!'

And then he kicked open the farmhouse door and sprinted out into the night.

'Oh, charming!' Amy called after him.

Jess darted towards the door, shouting after Chris, 'Come back! I can't leave Dad like this!'

But it was no use. Chris was gone.

Rory was helping Ralph Conway into an old armchair. The farmer winced as he sat down, one arm hanging limply. A gash on his forehead oozed blood.

But Rory was a trained nurse and knew what to look for. There didn't seem to be any serious damage, but you could never be totally sure with head injuries.

'He's in shock,' he said, peering into Ralph's eyes. They were heavy and a bit dazed. 'I think his arm could be broken too.'

Jess bit her lip, looking from her dad in the chair to the open door. She was torn between running after Chris and staying with her dad.

But there was never really any contest.

She joined Rory by her father's side as the rock monster tore its way through the room. Its hollow eyes scanned the room, searching for its prey.

Chapter 8

The Moon's Cold Gaze

The monster rose up to its full height with a loud, scraping roar.

Amy turned to the Doctor. 'Do something!'

But the Doctor's eyes were shining. 'No need,' he said.

'What?' said Amy, and she was joined in her gasp of disbelief by Rory and Jess.

The Doctor simply folded his arms and leant against a bookcase.

And did precisely nothing.

The rock monster stomped straight past him and smashed its way through the exit, taking a large part of the wall with it. It crunched its way out into the night and disappeared into the darkness.

'What's going on?' asked Amy, staring out through the ragged hole in the wall where the door had once been. 'Where's it going?'

'I'd say it was following Chris,' replied the Doctor. He peered out into the night. 'Wouldn't you?'

Everything had fallen unnaturally quiet. The monster was gone. All that was left was a trail of destruction through the farmhouse, bits and pieces of broken masonry and a lot of dust.

'It doesn't make sense,' said Amy. 'Why would the monster be following Chris?'

'Interesting, isn't it?' mused the Doctor.

'Interesting? It's madness!' Jess raised her voice. She stood up from where she had been kneeling by her father. 'I mean, it's just ridiculous. Why would it be following Chris?'

'That I do not know,' said the Doctor. He frowned thoughtfully. 'Yet.'

A lump of brick fell from the lintel over the doorway. Jess slumped in defeat. 'I just don't understand what's happening,' she moaned. 'What on Earth was that horrible thing?'

'That's what I intend to find out,' said the Doctor. He turned towards the wreckage of the doorway. 'Come on, Pond!'

Amy followed the Doctor out into the night, but he had already doubled back to speak to Rory.

'Stay here and look after Mr Conway and Jess,' he said.

Rory looked uncertain. 'What about the rock man? What if he comes back?'

'I doubt that'll happen. He's more interested in Chris Jenkins by the looks of it.'

'But –'

The Doctor sighed. 'Just sit tight here and look after Jess and her dad. They need you.'

'And you don't?'

'Yes – but I need you *here*.'

'Oh. Right. Well, OK.' Rory nodded. 'I'll stay here then.'

'Good man.'

The Doctor turned to leave once more, but Jess stopped him. 'Doctor – I need to know. Will Chris be all right?'

'We'll see,' the Doctor replied, as he slipped out into the darkness.

Chris was still running through the night. At first he had no idea where he was running to – he just had to get away. He had to get away from the insanity of the rock creature, from the Doctor and his friends, from

45

the farmhouse and from Jess.

Occasionally he glanced behind him. He could see the lights of the farmhouse, now in the distance. Above the dark buildings the moon shone brightly. The sight of it chilled him to the bone and made the breath catch in his throat.

Because, no matter how far he ran, Chris knew he would never escape the moon's cold gaze.

Behind Chris, unseen in the darkness, the rock creature trudged relentlessly across the moor.

Chapter 9

Follow the Rock

The Doctor could move very quickly when he had to
– one of the advantages of having a relatively young
body. He seemed to run in a tangle of arms and legs,
but he picked his way through the trees at quite a
pace regardless.

Amy struggled to keep up.

'Hang on!' she called.

The farmhouse was backed by trees, dark and
twisted in the night, almost impenetrable. Amy
couldn't understand how the Doctor could follow
anything through a forest at night.

'How do you know where we're going? I can't even
see that rock monster thingy!'

The Doctor hopped nimbly over a fallen tree trunk
and skidded to a halt. He was bouncing on his feet,
eager to continue with the chase. 'We don't need to see

him, Amy,' he said. 'We just follow the trail.'

'What trail?'

The Doctor pointed to the tree trunk. It looked like a thick, pale grey log in the moonlight.

But, as Amy watched, it started to grow paler by the second.

Eventually, with the softest crunch, it turned almost white. It looked as though it had been carved out of solid rock.

Moon rock.

'I don't believe it,' breathed Amy.

'Isn't it amazing?' The Doctor sounded delighted. 'The tree has turned to stone. Lunar stone.'

'But how?'

'Molecular reconfiguration. The creature touched the tree trunk and triggered the change. It did the same thing when it broke through Ralph Conway's wall last night – those stones weren't originally moon rock; they were *changed* into moon rock.'

Amy tried to make sense of it. 'You mean whatever that thing touches turns to moon rock?'

'Pretty much, yeah.'

'Why?'

'I've no idea. Maybe we could ask it – if we can catch it.'

They started off again, and now Amy could see

patches of white on the ground every so often, and the occasional stone tree or low-hanging branch perfectly reflecting the moonlight. These were the footsteps – or handprints – of the monster.

'Should be easy enough to track,' she admitted. But she hoped the monster didn't run too far – it was hard trying to keep up with the Doctor as he side-stepped and bounded his way out of the woods.

Before long they reached open ground – moor land. Mist covered the landscape like a thin, silvery sheet. It looked cold and unearthly – like the moon itself. Amy shivered.

The Doctor stopped and whipped out his sonic screwdriver. Its tip clicked open and glowed green as he used it to scan the area. After a few seconds he snapped it shut with a grunt of annoyance.

'It's gone!'

'Gone?'

The Doctor was clearly frustrated. 'Creature, trail, Chris – all gone. No trace of any molecular reconfiguration. It's just disappeared.'

'So what's happened? Has Chris been taken – abducted?'

The Doctor was down on his haunches now, scanning the ground with the sonic. 'It's a possibility,' he replied.

'Oh, no,' said Amy suddenly. 'I've just thought of another possibility.'

'What?'

'Anything the monster touches turns to stone, right?'

The Doctor stood up and frowned at her. 'Yes, right. What of it?'

'It touched Ralph Conway.'

Chapter 10

Changing

Rory pulled back the curtain and looked out of
the window.

The farmyard was moonlit and eerie – everything
was a pale grey colour and wreathed in a thin mist. The
dented Land Rover looked like a bone-white sculpture.

He could see the front door from this angle, if he
craned his neck a bit. The door was gone, smashed
into pieces, and the frame was splintered. But it was all
shining white in the darkness, as if it was carved out of
a piece of the moon.

He let the curtain drop back and turned to look at
Jess. 'How is he?'

Jess was sitting on the floor by her father. He was
in the armchair growing paler and greyer by the
minute. 'I think he's asleep,' she said quietly, 'or maybe
in a coma. I just can't tell.'

She was shivering. It was cold in the farmhouse now, with the doors bashed in front and back. Rory thought he could detect the first few tendrils of mist drifting in from outside. He took off his jacket and draped it over Jess's shoulders.

Ralph Conway was still breathing – just. It was shallow, barely visible, but he was definitely alive. Rory wasn't sure how much longer he would last, though. The ugly scar on his forehead looked raw. The rock monster had hit him hard.

'I don't even know if he can see me,' Jess said, waving a hand in front of Ralph's eyes. He continued to stare straight ahead.

'Probably concussion,' said Rory.

'Dad?' said Jess. 'Dad. Can you hear me?' There was no response. She turned to Rory. 'Shouldn't we call an ambulance or something?'

'Er, yes. Good idea.' Rory thought for a moment. 'Take a while to get here though. We're in the middle of nowhere.'

Jess nodded. 'We're a good hour's drive from the nearest hospital. But we could save some time if we drive him ourselves. Use the Land Rover.'

'That could be difficult. The monster totalled it.'

'What about Chris's car?'

Rory bit his lip. He was thinking about explaining

all of this to a tired medical doctor in casualty. He really didn't fancy the idea. 'Perhaps we're being a bit hasty, Jess . . . '

Jess gave a hiss of exasperation and turned back to her father. 'Dad! Wake up! It's me – Jess! Come on!' She turned back to Rory once more. 'Where's the Doctor? We need him here! He shouldn't have run off like that!'

'He's not that kind of doctor,' Rory said.

'Then what kind is he?'

'A sort of . . . outer space kind.'

'Don't be stupid,' Jess said angrily.

Rory could tell that she was frightened. And he knew how that felt. 'You saw that rock creature,' he said gently. 'You've seen the moon stones. Trust me, the Doctor will be able to sort it –'

But Jess was no longer listening. She had been distracted by something on her father's face. 'Rory – look!'

Ralph had suddenly turned very pale – almost white – as if the colour had been completely drained from his face. The skin looked dry and dusty.

'Oh, my goodness,' whispered Jess.

Rory peered closer. Then he swallowed. Ralph's eyes were open but grey and opaque.

Something was going horribly wrong.

Rory reached out to touch Ralph's hand. 'Mr Conway . . . ?'

'Don't touch him!' commanded the Doctor, striding into the room with Amy.

Rory jumped back as if stung and Jess gasped with relief. 'Doctor! Thank goodness – what's happening? Where's Chris?'

'He's gone,' the Doctor replied. He tried to make it sound as if this was perfectly OK, but his hands were clenched into fists. 'I'm sorry.'

'Gone?' Jess echoed. Her face had fallen. 'Where?'

'We don't know yet,' Amy said. 'We lost him in the fog. And the monster.'

'And that,' said the Doctor gravely, 'looks to be the least of our problems . . . '

He was staring hard at Ralph Conway, who sat stiffly in his chair, as grey and lifeless as a stone statue.

Chapter 11
A Nice Cup of Tea

The Doctor scanned Ralph with the sonic screwdriver.
The green glow passed over the stony features and
shone deep into the sightless eyes. Eventually the
whirring of the screwdriver ceased and the Doctor
flicked it open to inspect the readings.

'Well?' asked Jess. Amy could see that she was
worried sick. 'What's happened to him?'

There was a deep frown of concern on the Doctor's
face. 'Your dad's been turned to stone,' he said simply.
'Moon stone, to be precise.'

'But how?'

'The rock creature touched him, triggering a
complete molecular transformation . . .'

'I mean, how is that even *possible*?'

The Doctor looked closely at Jess. 'Anything's
possible,' he told her gently. 'Anything. Including getting

him changed back again to the way he was. The way he should be. From what I can tell, the transformation is highly unstable. It could be reversed.'

Jess wiped the tears from her eyes. 'I hope you know what you're doing, Doctor.'

'Of course I do.' The Doctor turned back to look at Ralph Conway. Unseen by Jess, the Doctor flashed a desperate look at Rory and Amy.

Rory cleared his throat. 'I'll make us all a cup of tea.'

'Yes!' the Doctor agreed. 'Perfect! Just what we all need. A nice cup of tea. Always helps me think . . .' He began to pace around the wreckage of the living room.

Amy was picking up some of the fallen chairs and ornaments. There was moon rock and dust everywhere, but she thought that it probably looked worse than it was. When everything was tidied up, they'd have a clearer idea of just how bad the damage to the farmhouse was.

The Doctor was thinking aloud. 'Whatever that rock creature was – oh, what shall we call him? The Rock Man?'

'The Moon Man?' suggested Rory.

'Moon Monster,' said Amy.

'Rock Man it is, then. Whatever it actually is, it can transform anything it touches into moon rock.

Some kind of sub-atomic virus, I should think. Or maybe quantum electron reversal. Or maybe . . . '

'I just want my dad back again,' interrupted Jess. 'Back to the way he was.'

The Doctor pointed a finger at her. 'Straight to the point. Good. Like that. Yes – but how do we change him back again?'

'We don't even know how he was changed in the first place,' Amy said. 'Or *why*.'

'Why?' Jess frowned.

The Doctor raised his finger. 'Good point, Amy. *Why* was the Rock Man changing things into moon stone? I mean, it seems to be unintentional. It didn't matter what the Rock Man touched, it was all transformed willy-nilly. Wall, car, door, furniture, even Ralph. So it seems to be an accidental side effect – it just can't help it.'

'Poor thing,' said Amy drily.

'It means there can't be any evolutionary purpose to it,' said the Doctor, thinking aloud. 'Which means that this creature isn't *natural*. It shouldn't exist . . .'

'But it does,' Rory pointed out.

'And this isn't helping get my dad back to normal,' Jess said. 'Isn't there anything you can do? What about that screwdriver thing?'

'It isn't a magic wand,' snapped the Doctor. 'I can't

just zap him back to normal. We've got to think this through.'

'But we've got to *do* something,' Jess insisted. There was panic in her voice now.

The Doctor looked closely into her eyes. 'Jess, I know you're worried – but trust me. I'll find a way.'

Jess's eyes filled with tears. 'What if he dies?'

'The molecular transformation is rapid but pretty unstable. If we can find a way to halt the process in time then we can reverse it.'

'And how do we do that?'

'That's a good question,' the Doctor admitted. He looked at Rory and Amy. 'Any suggestions?'

He was met by blank, fearful looks.

'No?' The Doctor looked upset for a moment. But then he clapped his hands together and smiled. 'Right then. All down to me. Hush while I think. Wait – did somebody mention a cup of tea?'

'That would be me,' said Rory.

Rory started to move towards the kitchen, but Amy suddenly let out a yelp of alarm. 'Wait – look!'

She was pointed at Ralph Conway, still frozen solid in his armchair.

'I thought I saw Mr Conway move.'

'Dad?' said Jess, bending closer. She peered into the grey, sightless eyes. 'Dad? Can you hear me?' she whispered. And then, despairingly: 'It's impossible. He's like a statue.'

'Keep away, Jess,' said the Doctor firmly.

'But –'

Rory pulled Jess gently back. 'Best not to get too close if the Doctor says so.'

But Rory himself had stepped closer to Ralph's chair. And in that second they all saw it happen – almost faster than the eye could follow, Ralph's stone hand leapt out towards Rory.

Chapter 12
Frozen

Ralph's grey hand closed around Rory's jacket. Rory tried to pull away, but the grip was like a vice. He struggled and pulled, but there was no getting free.

And then Rory's jacket began to turn to stone. It whitened, and the material stiffened –

'Rory!' Amy screamed.

In a last, desperate motion, Rory twisted and turned and slipped his arms out of the jacket – just as it completed its transformation into moon rock. Held at arm's length by Ralph, the jacket immediately began to crack under its own weight. In an instant it fell to bits, scattering across the floor like a piece of dropped china.

And by now, Ralph was up and moving. He stood stiffly, with an unearthly scrape of rock moving against rock. His head turned slowly to watch Rory as he cowered away, clinging to Amy. The colourless stone eyes seemed to narrow.

Jess was screaming. The sight of her father turned to stone was bad enough. Seeing him get up and move was almost worse.

Ralph was utterly blind to her distress. His attention was focused entirely on Rory and Amy.

The Doctor stepped up behind Ralph and aimed his sonic screwdriver. The tip flashed a brilliant green and a high-pitched whine filled the air, but there seemed to be no effect on the statue-like figure. The Doctor quickly tried several different settings, and eventually the statue's head twitched around to look at him.

'That's got your attention,' said the Doctor.

With a dull scraping noise, Ralph Conway turned and walked purposefully towards the Doctor.

'That's right – follow the pretty green light . . .' The Doctor backed away, reversing out of the room, back towards the kitchen. He held the sonic screwdriver up, its emerald glow illuminating the darkened farmhouse.

Ralph followed him with heavy footsteps. The Doctor climbed backwards up a kitchen chair, onto the remains of the table, and out through the smashed doorway.

Ralph swept aside the wreckage and followed him outside.

The Doctor was in the farmyard now. Mist curled around his boots as he backed away from the Rock Man.

In the moonlight, Ralph Conway looked like a grim, white avenger. His pitiless gaze never left the Doctor as he trudged after him.

The Doctor circled around the farmer's Land Rover. That, too, resembled a stone carving – having been transformed into moon rock by the original Rock Man.

The Doctor sidestepped nimbly, putting the Land Rover between himself and Ralph. The farmer banged a stone fist down on the vehicle's bonnet in annoyance, cracking it like he had a sculptor's chisel.

The Doctor guessed it wouldn't take much for Ralph to smash the Land Rover into bits or just climb over it. He had to do something quickly. With a deft movement, he changed the frequency of the screwdriver again and aimed it squarely at Ralph.

The sonic screwdriver screamed and Ralph instantly froze.

'You did it!' Amy cried in relief. They had all followed them out of the house.

'Good old screwdriver,' said Rory. 'If you ask me, it is a bit magic.'

'Not magic,' snapped the Doctor. 'Just a carefully

judged frequency modulation. The sound waves are vibrating the stone to a point where it cannot move. If I adjust the frequency by just one megahertz, the stone will shatter into a million pieces – and it's goodbye, Ralph.'

'Dad!' moaned Jess. 'Oh, Doctor – be careful!'

'I'm being *extremely* careful.' The Doctor moved cautiously forward, adjusting his grip on the screwdriver. 'But I can't keep him frozen like this all night. Rory, Amy – get some rope, anything you can, and see if you can tie him up.'

Rory went straight to the Land Rover, expecting to find a tow rope. But the vehicle was solid rock. There was no way to open it – and even then, he thought glumly, the contents might also have turned to stone.

'Try the shed,' said Amy, heading for the old wooden lean-to built against the farmhouse. Inside there were a number of tools – spades, garden forks, some musty cardboard boxes and a spare hosepipe. Coiled up on a hook was a long, blue, nylon washing line.

'Perfect,' said the Doctor.

Amy and Rory set about winding the line around Ralph's wrists and ankles, stretching it back and forth until he appeared to be caught in a giant, bright blue spider web.

'Be careful,' the Doctor said. He still had the sonic

trained on Ralph. 'One crack and he could shatter.'

'What if he sort of . . . topples over?' Rory asked. 'Once you switch off the sonic he's free to move. But he's all tied up now and he might fall flat on his face.'

'Could be nasty,' agreed Amy.

Jess appeared, carrying a long length of heavy chain. She was shaking, tears streaking her face, but she was determined to stop any harm coming to her father. 'We can use this chain to secure him. If we wrap it around him a few times and then around the Land Rover, it should stop him falling over.'

They got to work and a little while later, with sore hands covered in rusty smears, they had secured Ralph to the Land Rover. The whole thing looked like some kind of weird modern art sculpture.

The Doctor clicked the sonic screwdriver off. The sudden silence seemed strange and frightening. Ralph Conway struggled to move – but was held fast by the nylon rope and chains.

The Doctor walked up to Ralph.

The Rock Man stared impassively back.

'Can you talk?' asked the Doctor.

But there was no reply.

'Might as well be talking to a statue . . .' muttered the Doctor.

The Rock Man continued to stare at the Doctor.

Then it turned its head slowly to look at Jess and the others.

'He doesn't even recognise me,' said Jess sadly. 'There's nothing in his eyes. Just nothing.'

'He's not your father anymore,' the Doctor said.

'But can you turn him back again?'

'I don't know, Jess,' replied the Doctor honestly. 'I just don't know.'

Chapter 13

Safety in Sunshine

They returned to the kitchen in a grave mood. 'Just look at this place,' said Jess despairingly.

The farmhouse was a wreck. There was broken furniture, crockery and fragments of moon rock everywhere.

'Yes,' said the Doctor eagerly. '*Look* at this place. Notice *everything*.'

'I think Jess is a bit upset, Doctor,' sighed Amy. The Doctor could seem so insensitive at times, it was embarrassing.

'Oh, don't worry about the farmhouse,' the Doctor told Jess. 'Bit of a tidy-up, lick of paint, you won't notice,' he ended lamely. 'Well, OK, maybe it'll need a bit more than that – but think of it as an opportunity. Maybe it was time you redecorated anyway. I mean, look at that wallpaper . . .' The Doctor pulled a disgusted face.

'Not helping, Doctor . . . ' whispered Amy.

Jess was just staring out of the window at her father.

Ralph Conway continued to pull and twist against his bonds.

The sky above was turning a strange colour. It was that time of night known as the false dawn – when things appear to be getting lighter, but sunrise is still an hour or so away.

The Doctor, Amy and Rory were trying to tidy up the mess. Jess didn't seem interested.

'She's more concerned about her dad,' Rory told the Doctor quietly.

'I know. And quite right, too. But still . . .' He turned on his heel, letting his sharp gaze wander over the debris in the kitchen. 'Look at this place. Notice everything. There's something I'm missing.'

'A clue?'

'It's not *Scooby Doo*, Rory.' Suddenly the Doctor banged the flat of his hand against the side of his head. 'Think, Doctor, think! Rory – cup of tea. Come on! I need tea to think. And biscuits – plenty of biscuits!'

Without another word the Doctor stalked out of the kitchen and plonked himself down in one of the armchairs in the living room. Then he closed his eyes and began to snore loudly.

'This is hardly the time for a snooze,' grumbled Rory.

'I'm thinking,' replied the Doctor, without opening his eyes.

'And snoring?'

'That's not snoring – that's the gears going round in my brain. Now shush and go and make that pot of tea.'

Rory went back into the kitchen where Amy met him with a frown. 'This place really is a mess. The Doctor's right, furniture can be replaced and walls can be repaired – but the dust is awful. It's absolutely everywhere. Look at my hands!'

She held them out for Rory to see. They were completely grey.

'Is is safe to touch the dust like that?' wondered Rory. 'Shouldn't you wear gloves or something?'

'The dust itself is completely harmless,' the Doctor called from his armchair in the other room. He still had his eyes shut.

'But it's so . . . sticky,' said Amy. 'It gets everywhere and stays there!'

Suddenly the Doctor leapt out of his seat and catapulted himself into the kitchen. 'Wait! Did you say it's sticky?'

He grabbed Amy's wrists and inspected her hands

closely. 'Well, not *sticky*,' she said. 'Not sticky like a sweet or a lollipop is sticky. But it just sort of gets everywhere and coats everything . . .'

'Yes, of course,' said the Doctor, turning her hands this way and that.

Then he dropped to all fours and hunted around for some dust of his own. There was plenty. In another moment he was rubbing some of the fine grey dust between his own finger and thumb.

'Is there a problem?' wondered Jess.

The Doctor licked a finger and smacked his lips. 'Definitely moon dust. And yet . . .'

'I can't make a cup of tea with this,' complained Rory, holding up the kettle. 'It's covered in dust and it won't even rinse off.'

'That's it!' exclaimed the Doctor, leaping to his feet. He snatched the kettle from Rory. 'The dust is electrostatic. It carries a tiny, tiny electrical charge. Enough for each particle to be attracted to anything else nearby. I mean, moon dust – it's famous for it. How could I forget?'

'Perhaps you're not perfect after all?' Rory suggested gently.

The Doctor shot him a look. 'Don't be silly. Electrostatic dust. The astronauts on the *Apollo* missions had a terrible time with it. Got absolutely everywhere. Stuck to their boots, the joints on their spacesuits, moving parts on the lunar rovers. Nightmare.'

'But what does it mean?' asked Amy. 'We already know it's moon dust, after all. Comes from the moon rock, which is pretty much everywhere around here at the moment.'

The Doctor peered at her. 'Yes. Yes it is, isn't it?'

'So, what . . . ?' Rory prompted, taking the kettle back.

'Makes you wonder, doesn't it?' replied the Doctor with a curious smile.

'Wonder what?'

'If it's an invasion.'

'If what's an invasion?'

'All this!' the Doctor gestured grandly around them at the farmhouse wreckage. 'Perhaps this is some kind of alien invasion.'

'Oh, you'd love that, wouldn't you?' Amy said.

'No, wait, it can't be,' the Doctor said, suddenly changing his mind. His face fell. 'Pity though. At least then I'd know what was happening.'

'If it *was* an alien invasion,' said Rory, 'then they'd need to set their sights a little higher, wouldn't you say? I mean, no disrespect to Jess and her dad, but invading a small farm in the middle of England isn't exactly

Independence Day all over again, is it?'

'Don't forget *War of the Worlds* started on Horsell Common – at least it did in the original H.G. Wells book.'

'Yeah, but that was just a story.'

The Doctor frowned. 'Was it?'

Rory looked doubtful. 'Well, yeah, At least I thought it was.' Living with the Doctor meant that he was now prepared to believe in almost anything.

The Doctor broke into a grin. 'Yeah, course it was a story. Only joking. Old H.G. Wells loved a good joke. Met him once, you know.'

'Really?' Rory was impressed. 'What was he like?'

'Bit of a pain to be honest. Gave him a few ideas for *The Time Machine* though.'

'I bet you did.'

'On the other hand,' the Doctor went on, '*Independence Day* actually *did* happen – but not until 2109 your time.'

'Oh.' Rory was frowning now. He never knew when the Doctor was pulling his leg.

'Doctor – look at this!' Jess was by the kitchen window. She pointed to where the Land Rover and her father stood outside, still bound by chains and washing line.

They gathered at the window. The sun was just

coming up, sending rays of deep orange light across the dawn sky.

As the morning light touched the stone Ralph Conway, he seemed to flinch slightly.

'It's almost like the sunlight's hurting him,' said Jess.

'Not hurting him,' the Doctor said. 'Changing him. Look!'

Ralph had been struggling against his bonds. But now, as the first golden light of the new day touched his stone features, the man stopped moving. In minutes he was as lifeless as any statue.

The Doctor was already running out into the yard for a closer look. He circled around Ralph, watching for the slightest sign of movement.

Eventually, cautiously, he drew closer. Ralph didn't move.

The other joined him. 'Is he safe to be near?' asked Rory.

'Perfectly,' beamed the Doctor. 'It all makes sense now.'

'It does?' Jess didn't seem sure.

'Negative electrostatics,' nodded the Doctor.

'That's easy for you to say,' Rory smiled.

'It's a bit of a mouthful but that's how it works,' the Doctor replied. 'That's how the Rock Man can move around – and how Ralph can still move, even though he's made of stone. But ultraviolet light – such as sunshine – cancels the effect. Freezes the atoms where they are, so the thing's *completely* motionless.' The Doctor rapped his knuckles on Ralph's forehead.

'Hey,' said Jess. 'That's my dad you're tapping on the head.'

'I know.'

'You called him a "thing".'

'Sorry. Won't happen again.'

'Did you say ultraviolet light?' said Rory slowly. He was puzzling over something.

'Yeah. Sunlight. UV rays bombard the moon rock and –' the Doctor made a curious wriggling motion in the air with his fingers, '*Phhzzzzp*! Something amazing happens. But it means the Rock Men can only be active at night. During the day they're harmless.'

'Chris said he was researching into the effects of UV rays on certain kinds of minerals,' said Rory.

The Doctor clicked his fingers. 'That's it. That's it! Rory, you're wonderful. Amy, tell Rory he's wonderful.'

'You're wonderful,' Amy mouthed at Rory with a wink.

'I know,' he mouthed back.

'Now don't get all soppy on me,' warned the

Doctor. 'I'm thinking and soppy stuff gets in the way of me thinking.'

'And what, exactly, are you thinking about?' asked Amy.

'That I need to speak to Chris, right now.'

'But we don't even know if he managed to get away from the monster.'

The Doctor huffed impatiently. 'He better have!'

Jess was already trying her mobile phone. 'There's no answer. It's not even connecting to Chris's mobile – like there's a signal problem or something. That's not unusual around here, I'm afraid. But, if he is still alive, I've a good idea where he'll be.'

Chapter 14

The Research Centre

The sports car skidded to a halt and Amy flicked a strand of red hair out of her eyes. 'Not a bad ride,' she said.

The Doctor turned off the engine and smiled at her. 'Bit cramped,' he said. 'I prefer things to be slightly roomier on the inside.'

But the Doctor had, of course, relished the chance to drive Chris's car. 'It's only fair – he might want it back, after all,' was how he had explained it to Amy as he vaulted gleefully into the leather bucket seat behind the steering wheel.

The morning sunlight glinted off the red paintwork as they climbed out of the car. It was going to be a beautiful day – hopefully. Amy couldn't stop thinking about Ralph Conway. How did it feel to be turned into stone? Did he know what was happening? Did he know they were trying to help him?

Amy stretched her legs. It certainly had been a tight fit in that car. The Doctor had parked alongside a chain-link fence backed by thick bushes. There was no way to see what was on the other side and no sign of an entrance.

'Are you sure this is the right place?' Amy asked.

The Doctor pointed at a sign attached to the fence, half hidden by the foliage. It said:

HENSON RESEARCH CENTRE
NO UNAUTHORISED ACCESS
TRESPASSERS WILL BE PROSECUTED

'Not very welcoming,' commented Amy. She watched as the Doctor examined the fence. 'I suppose you'll want a leg up or something.'

'Something,' nodded the Doctor. He aimed his sonic screwdriver at the fence and the tip flashed green. A section of the chain-link quickly untwined and parted like a doorway.

The Doctor switched off the screwdriver and smiled. 'After you!'

Amy stepped through the gap and the Doctor followed.

'Don't you think a big hole in their fence could be regarded as suspicious?'

'What hole?' asked the Doctor innocently, as he used the sonic to meld the links back together, zipping up the gap behind them.

'I sometimes think that thing must be magic,' said Amy, as the Doctor spun the sonic screwdriver and dropped it back into his pocket with a flourish.

'Or just superior technology,' he said. 'Amounts to the same thing to the untrained eye. It's simply a case of vibrating the wires in the chain link at the correct frequency to open them, and then reversing the polarity to close them.'

'Like I said – magic.'

'A pair of sliding doors would look like magic to a caveman.'

Amy raised her eyebrows. 'Oh, thanks – I'm no better than a caveman now, am I?'

'Well, you humans have come a long way in the last few million years, but it pays not to get above yourselves.'

'Charming!'

The Doctor led the way through the bushes. 'Stop grumbling, Pond! Come and look at this!'

They emerged from the bushes by a tarmac path leading past a low, brick-built building. It was clean and modern, but with very few windows.

They crept quickly around the corner to a car park and a pair of large glass front doors. There was no one visible in the entrance foyer.

'That's odd – no receptionist and no security guards,' noted Amy. 'And yet there are cars in the car park.'

'It looks deserted,' agreed the Doctor, cupping his hands around his eyes as he peered in through the glass. 'Place like this should be busy. Lots of expensive equipment and top scientists – no one wants them standing idle.'

Amy pushed one of the doors open. 'It's not even locked.'

The Doctor followed her inside, ignoring the vacant reception desk, and went straight through the foyer to the double doors at the rear. 'Hello!' he called down the corridor beyond. There was no reply.

'Doesn't look like there's anyone home,' said Amy.

The Doctor pushed open a door leading to an office. It was empty. Then he tried another door, this one marked with the word 'LABORATORIES'.

Beyond it was another corridor, this one lined with doors leading to various research labs. Each one had its own strange label.

'Spectography, mineralogy, geochemistry . . .' Amy

read the signs on each door before opening them to reveal large rooms full of scientific equipment – but no people.

Computers whirred and indicator lights flickered on a variety of machines – but there was no one to read the gauges or take down the readings.

'It's like the *Marie Celeste*,' Amy said. 'Everyone's just . . . disappeared!'

'I hope not,' said the Doctor. 'I visited the *Marie Celeste*. I don't want to go through all that again.'

Amy pushed open a door marked "UV Biochemistry". 'Um, Doctor, I think you'd better see this . . .'

Like the other labs, this room was full of scientific apparatus – work benches, computers and other complex machinery. There were a number of people – scientists, Amy presumed – seated at the various workstations and equipment.

But none of them were alive.

The Doctor stepped cautiously into the lab.

Hardly daring to breathe, Amy stayed in the doorway. The scene looked so strange and terrible that she didn't want to even enter the room.

The scientists stood peering into microscopes, or sitting at computer keyboards, utterly lifeless and unmoving – every one of them turned to stone.

'Just like Ralph Conway,' whispered Amy.

The Doctor was moving from scientist to scientist, checking them with his sonic screwdriver.

'No electrostatic activity at all,' he said grimly. 'They're completely motionless – dormant.'

Despite the Doctor's reassuring tone, Amy stayed in the doorway, unwilling to walk into what suddenly felt like a graveyard.

And then a heavy hand fell on her shoulder.

Chapter 15
Waiting

Rory was helping Jess to tidy up at the farmhouse.
They had moved a lot of the rubble and moon stone
and dumped it in the yard. Rory had picked up most
of the broken furniture and put back anything that
was usable where it belonged. The rest, the remains of
it, he threw into the yard.

'You know, it's not as bad as it looks,' he told
Jess, as he brushed the last chips of moon rock into
a bin bag.

She raised an eyebrow. 'Really?'

'Most of this stuff is OK,' Rory said. 'The walls
need a bit of rebuilding and re-plastering, but nothing
a couple of good decorators couldn't handle in a day
or so. And the rest . . . well, it just needs cleaning up.'

Jess sank into a chair. 'I hope you're right.'

Rory tied the bin bag and swung it out of the back

door. 'You watch. By the time the Doctor and Amy get back, this place will look fine.' He hesitated, seeing that Jess wasn't convinced. 'Tell you what, let's take a break and have some breakfast.'

Rory found a toaster and a loaf of bread and set to work. Jess joined him in the kitchen, staring out of the window at her father. He still stood by the Land Rover, little more than a statue.

'Isn't there anything we can do for him?' she wondered.

'Not that I know of,' Rory replied. 'Maybe when the Doctor gets back . . .'

'Maybe we should have taken him to a hospital or something.'

'I don't think that would help. Believe me, I'd know – I'm a nurse. I used to spend all my time in hospitals and never once did I see anyone brought in because they'd been turned into moon rock. No one would have a clue what to do. Except the Doctor.'

'You really think he can help?'

'There's no one else I'd rather trust.'

Jess let out a sigh. 'I thought I could trust Chris – and look what happened there.'

'Don't be too hard on him,' Rory said gently. 'He was scared.'

'We all were – but he's the only one who ran away.'

84

Rory shrugged. 'Maybe that just shows he's cleverer than the rest of us. I wish I'd thought of it.'

'Don't joke. I'm supposed to be marrying him, remember.'

'People do a lot of stupid things before they get married,' Rory said, with some feeling. 'Don't be too hard on him.'

'Maybe Dad was right. Maybe he isn't right for me.'

'Anything's possible,' Rory said. 'But at the end of the day, it's not your dad who's marrying him. It's you. Only you can decide.'

Chapter 16

What Went Wrong?

The hand felt unnaturally heavy. Amy spun around with a yelp, expecting to see the Rock Man towering over her.

But all she saw was Chris Jenkins.

He looked tense and scared – almost as much as Amy. His face was pale and drawn, with dark circles under his eyes.

'You just frightened the life out of me!' Amy yelled, swatting his hand aside. She felt relieved and angry at the same time. It didn't help that she could hear the Doctor laughing softly behind her.

'Look out!' the Doctor said, miming a big scary monster. 'It's *Chris*!'

Amy aimed a blow at his shoulder. 'Hate you.'

'Chris, glad you're here,' the Doctor said, moving past her and shaking Chris by the hand. He looked dazed and confused as the Doctor peered closely into his eyes, as if searching for something deep within.

'Doctor . . . Amy . . .' Chris mumbled. 'How did you get here?'

'Oh, that was easy. Your sports car. Love it! Goes like the clappers, lovely motor.'

A frown twitched into view on Chris's forehead. 'How's Jess? Is she all right?'

'Yes, she's fine – apart from the fact that her dad's been turned to stone.' The Doctor looked around the lab again. 'A bit like your friends here.' He turned back to Chris, a steely look in his deep set eyes. 'Care to tell us about it?'

'Um, yeah. Yeah. That would be good.'

'So all that talk about analysing rock samples and handling moon rock – you knew something was already wrong,' said Amy a little later. They were sitting in a side room around a coffee table. It was some kind of rest area for the scientists, with a drinks machine and a small snooker table.

'Yeah,' Chris replied, sipping coffee from a polystyrene cup. He stared at the table in front of him. 'I'm afraid so.'

'Why didn't you speak up, then?' Amy demanded. She was annoyed with him. 'At the farmhouse. You could have said.'

'I was scared. I don't really understand what's going on – you see, I think it might be all my fault.'

'Why?'

'Part of the research we do here . . . well, there was a project, investigating the effects of UV rays on various kinds of rock.' Chris sighed and ran a hand down over his face. 'Including moon rock samples. It's something to do with NASA's preparations for the next moon landings. They need to control dust contamination. Our research was important – and top secret. I didn't want to start chatting all about it to strangers.'

'But still – even when that Rock Man attacked us . . .'

'I panicked. I just wanted to get away.'

'And you wanted to draw it away from Jess Conway,' interjected the Doctor. He was potting a red on the snooker table. The tip of the cue clicked against the ball and it shot straight into the corner pocket. 'Because you knew what it was after.'

The Doctor straightened up, rubbed the end of his cue with a piece of blue chalk attached by a string to the table, and smiled gently. 'You knew it was coming after you.'

Chris closed his eyes. 'When we started the experiments, the results were completely unexpected.

The moon dust reacted in ways we couldn't have guessed at . . .'

'Electrostatic animation, cross-polarisation of the electrons at atomic level,' said the Doctor quickly. 'Yes, worked out all that for myself. The question is – what went wrong?'

'I don't know.'

The Doctor potted another red with a rattling stroke of his cue. 'Oh, come on, Chris. You must have a clue.'

'The moon rock had to be handled with extreme caution at all times,' Chris said. 'The samples were kept in sealed cases. We handled them using gloves inside an airtight box. All the normal precautions. But one day . . . one of the insulated gloves tore. It must have been a sharp edge on one of the rock samples. I'm not sure. But the seal was broken.'

'That wouldn't normally be a problem,' remarked the Doctor thoughtfully, lining up another shot. 'Moon rock is pretty harmless.'

'That's what we thought. But we were wrong.'

'The people in the lab,' realised Amy sadly. 'Were they . . . infected or something?'

'Mutated,' Chris replied. 'It was horrible. Slowly at first – everyone was aware that they were getting heavier, stiffer . . . and then suddenly . . .'

'Sudden organic molecular reconfiguration,' finished the Doctor. He had cleared the table. He carefully placed the snooker cue back on the green baize surface. 'They never stood a chance.'

'And neither did Ralph,' said Amy.

Chris's head jerked up. 'What?'

'The Rock Man touched him, remember. Triggered the molecular change thingy.'

'Oh, no,' Chris buried his face in his hands. 'Not Ralph . . . What must Jess be thinking?' He stood up. 'I have to see her. She'll be distraught. Her dad's all she's got . . .'

'Wait a minute,' said the Doctor. 'Jess is OK. Her dad is OK – for the moment. The effect is unstable and I think the process can be reversed. But I need to know more about how it happened.'

Chris drew a deep breath. 'All right. What can I do?'

'Show us where the real work was done,' replied the Doctor without missing a beat.

Amy frowned. 'But I thought that was the lab . . .'

The Doctor shook his head. 'The work you say you were doing here – it would require at the very least a UV laser set-up, positively charged electron chambers and a nuclear particle tracker. There's nothing like the equipment necessary in there –

and certainly no sealed unit.' He swung his gaze around to face Chris. 'So, come on, out with it: where's the top secret lab?'

Chapter 17

Hoggett's Offer

There was a knock at the farmhouse door – or what remained of it.

'I'll get it,' said Rory. He went out to the kitchen and found a large, overweight man with a very red face standing in the doorway.

'Hoggett,' said the man as Rory appeared.

'I'm sorry . . . ?' Rory said.

'Who the Devil are you?' the man demanded, his thick eyebrows drawing down over a pair of small, but very sharp, eyes.

'Er . . . I'm Rory. I'm just visiting.'

'Where's Conway?'

Rory glanced out into the farmyard, where Ralph Conway stood immobile by the Land Rover.

'Come on, boy, spit it out,' demanded the man. 'He must be here somewhere. Tell him I want to see him!'

'Dad's not available right now,' said Jess, joining Rory. Her voice was cool, and Rory immediately got the impression that neither Jess or this rude visitor liked each other.

'This is Mr Hoggett,' Jess told Rory. 'You could say he's our next-door neighbour. He owns the farm across the valley. And the farm next to that. And three farms beyond that.'

'Four,' Hoggett corrected. 'And it'll be five when I get this place.'

'And we keep telling you,' said Jess icily, 'that this farm isn't for sale.'

'It might not be on the market,' agreed Hoggett. 'But that doesn't mean it can't be bought.'

'My dad has already told you to back off, Mr Hoggett. We're not interested.'

'Well, we'll see about that,' said Hoggett. 'I've come to make a new offer. One that even someone as stubborn as your father would be hard pushed to refuse.'

'Look,' said Rory. 'This isn't a good time. As you can see . . . we've had a bit of bother and . . .'

Hoggett looked quickly around the kitchen, taking in the broken table, chairs, plasterboard and door frame. 'I can see that, boy. I'm not blind. And that's exactly why I've come. It'll cost a damned fortune to rebuild this place . . . money I know Conway doesn't have. If he can't afford to pay any workers, then he can't afford to pay for the upkeep of this place.'

'He'll find a way,' Jess argued – but she didn't sound convinced.

'Rubbish,' Hoggett scoffed. 'The place is falling apart – look around you!' He glanced around the kitchen and seemed surprised to find just how bad a state it was in. 'I mean, *look* at it! Place is falling apart!'

'Really,' Rory said, as firmly as he could manage. 'This isn't the right time.'

Hoggett gave him a withering look. 'I've come to speak to the organ grinder, boy – not one of his monkeys. Where is Conway? Don't tell me he's left you two in charge?'

'Dad isn't here at the moment,' Jess said patiently. 'Maybe if you could come back another time–'

'I'm not available at your father's beck and call, girl. Frankly I find it astonishing that Conway should leave the farm under the management of a young girl like you and her boyfriend.'

Jess glanced at Rory. 'Rory isn't my boyfriend.'

'I'm not her boyfriend,' Rory confirmed, just so there was no possibility of confusion.

Hoggett peered at him closely, lip curling. 'Oh, no. You're not. I'm thinking of that other oaf from town.

Whatshisname. Jenkins. Always hanging around like a bad smell.'

'There's no call for that,' said Rory. He was beginning to get very fed up with this horrible man.

'Does *he* know you're seeing this fellow as well?' Hoggett asked Jess, jerking a thumb at Rory.

'I keep telling you, I'm not her boyfriend,' protested Rory. 'I'm not anyone's boyfriend. I'm married. To Amy Pond.'

'What are you blathering on about, boy? Sounds like you don't know what you're talking about half the time.'

'Perhaps you should just go.'

Hoggett seethed for a moment. 'Well, I can see it's pointless staying here unless I can speak to Conway.' He turned to Jess. 'Tell your father this is his final chance. He won't get a better offer. And tell him that statue he's had erected in the yard is damned ridiculous.'

'Statue?'

'Yes – the one with him chained to a Land Rover. Never seen anything like it! Damned ridiculous waste of money. The man's got far too high an opinion of himself.' Hoggett let out a loud *harrumph*. 'I never had a statue made of *me*.'

And with that, Hoggett turned and left without another word, stomping over the last bits of brick and dust left in the broken doorway. He stalked away across the yard, shot a dark look at Ralph Conway's "statue", and climbed into his Range Rover.

Jess watched him go and wiped a tear from her tired eyes.

'Don't get upset,' Rory said. 'He's just a . . . horrible man. Ignore him.'

'I can't ignore him, Rory. He's right. We can't afford to run this farm on our own. There's too much work to do for two people and we'd struggle to pay anyone to work here, even if they'd come out from the town.'

'I can see things were already difficult before . . . all this.'

'Dad knows he's going to have to sell the farm. He's not getting any younger. But he refuses to sell it to Hoggett. He practically owns the whole valley now.'

'I'm sure your dad will think of something.'

Jess smiled weakly. 'Thanks. I know you're trying to help, and you're very sweet.' She squeezed Rory's hand. 'Amy is a very lucky girl.'

Chapter 18
Minus Seven

'The research centre extends far below ground level,' Chris explained. 'In fact, two-thirds of it is underground. The really top secret stuff – high level, fringe science research and development – takes place down on level Minus Seven.'

'That sounds brilliant,' said the Doctor, rubbing his hands together. He looked like a child about to walk into a sweet shop. 'Fringe science – my favourite kind!'

'What's fringe science?' asked Amy.

'All the sort of research that's on the very edge of known science,' Chris answered. They were walking along one of the corridors at the rear of the research centre, heading for the lifts that would take them down to level Minus Seven.

'All the stuff that's on the *fringe* of twenty-first century human science,' the Doctor corrected. He winked at Amy. 'They'll get there eventually.'

'I beg your pardon?'

'Nothing! Lead on.'

Chris stopped at the lifts, his shoulders slumping. 'There's really not much point. There's a problem I haven't told you about. The main lab on Minus Seven is locked and sealed.'

'Oh, that sounds even more interesting,' smiled the Doctor.

Chris, pale and sweating, met the Doctor's gaze. 'Doctor – you really, really don't want to go down there.'

But the Doctor's eyes were shining with curiosity now. 'Yes, I really, really do.'

They went down in the lift to level Minus Seven. There was a short, bare corridor leading to a set of heavy double doors. Each had a circular window made from frosted glass with the research company's logo etched into it.

'Not much of a barrier,' sniffed the Doctor, waving his sonic screwdriver casually at the doors. They clicked open immediately.

Amy screwed her eyes up as a gust of cold, dead air escaped with a quiet hiss. Beyond was a darkened concrete passage.

They stepped into the passage. Amy shivered. 'It's so cold down here – with all this concrete.'

The Doctor touched the wall. 'Not concrete, Amy – moon rock. The whole corridor is made from moon rock.'

'We shouldn't be here,' said Chris nervously.

'This is *exactly* where we should be,' the Doctor insisted.

He used the sonic screwdriver to light the way. It was very gloomy and at one point Amy stubbed her toe on something lying near the wall. 'Ouch!'

The Doctor shone the light on the floor, revealing a huddled grey shape. At first it looked just like a large rock or a stone, but then they saw that it was actually in the shape of a man – crawling along the floor. His face was frozen in a mask of fear.

'Oh, no,' Amy whispered.

The Doctor examined the stone body. 'Someone trying to escape,' he said quietly. 'Caught in the same transformation wave that turned this whole corridor to moon stone.'

'I told you it was a bad idea to come down here,' Chris said. 'We should go back now.'

'No,' said Amy. She tried to hide the shake in her voice. 'We've come this far. We have to find out what's going on.'

The Doctor smiled at her in the darkness and squeezed her hand. 'Come on, Pond,' he said.

Chris followed the Doctor and Amy to the far end of the passageway. Here there was a pair of heavy steel doors – or at least, they had once been steel. Now, they were rock. Grey stone rivets ran along the edges and the circular windows were useless.

'It's locked solid,' said Chris. 'There is no way through.'

The Doctor scanned it with the sonic screwdriver. 'All the internal electronics and locks have been turned to moon stone . . .' He fiddled with the screwdriver and pointed it at the centre of the doors. The tip glowed a fierce green. 'However – if I can break down the machinery . . .'

The sonic pitch rose to a scream and suddenly there was a series of heavy clunks and cracks from within the doors.

And a dark, black split appeared between them.

'Come on – brute force now.' The Doctor dug his fingers into the split and started to heave.

Amy joined him, while Chris pulled at the other door.

The stone doors ground slowly aside, releasing a cascade of fine grey dust over the Doctor's head and shoulders. When they had forced the doors open just wide enough to step through, Amy giggled. 'That's quite a dandruff problem you've got there, Doctor.'

The Doctor brushed the dust from his hair and stared into the cold darkness beyond the doors. 'It's like opening a grave,' he said quietly.

Chris was shaking like a leaf. The Doctor aimed his torchlight through the gap – and Amy let out a sharp cry of despair.

Chapter 19

Stone Science

The huge, underground laboratory was impressive enough, but not exactly unexpected.

What took Amy by surprise was that everything – every computer, workstation, cable, monitor and control panel, right down to the last button and rivet – was made out of solid rock.

She had never seen anything like this. It looked like the world's most incredible, most complicated sculpture.

At the centre of the chamber was some kind of apparatus shaped like a giant, upturned spider. There was a round, central machine covered with technological components, with a number of thick support girders radiating out and up towards the ceiling.

The whole thing was surrounded by a number of heavy cables and power lines that trailed across the floor, plugged into various sockets and machines.

The Doctor stepped straight into the stone laboratory, his boots echoing around the cathedral-like space. His torchlight roved around the pale rock, picking out controls, computer banks – and then a man's face.

Amy gasped again – and then realised that, of course, the man was made out of rock. As still and lifeless as everything else down here.

'I'll never look at the moon in the same way again,' she said.

The Doctor examined the stone man. 'Caught in the transformation wave. Just like the others upstairs.'

'Did any of the scientists survive?' Amy asked Chris.

He shook his head. 'I'm the only one.'

The Doctor had moved to one of the main workstations. He scanned the computer with his sonic screwdriver, the green light playing eerily over the rocky surface. 'Everything is stored in here, all the research data, experiments, everything. But it's all turned to rock. The hard drives and flash memory – *everything* is rock.'

'Going to be hard to access any of the data, then,' Amy realised.

'Hard – but not impossible. There are some civilisations, mainly in the Pron-Kalunka Galaxy, that use granite as the base matter for all their technology.'

'And it works?'

'Yes, but it's very slow and a bit on the heavy side.' The Doctor knelt down, examining the edge of one of the computers very closely. 'But it does work. If I can just remove one of these memory sticks, I'm sure I could find a way to get the data out . . .'

'I don't like it down here,' Chris said. 'It all happened so quickly. The transformation was so fast . . . I was lucky not to be here when it happened.'

'Where were you?' Amy asked.

Chris gave a humourless laugh. 'I'd gone to start up the UV generators. They're located in a side-room in the basement. It's not far from here – but far enough.'

The Doctor looked up, frowning. 'Start up the UV generators? That was lucky.'

'Not really.' Chris shuddered as he remembered. 'I heard it happen. Heard the shouts – the terrible grinding, cracking noise as anything and everything down here turned to stone. When I came back, I couldn't believe my eyes.'

'What did you do?'

'Ran around the research centre in a panic. No one else here was left alive.'

'What about the other scientists or their families and friends?' asked Amy. 'Didn't anyone enquire?'

'You have to understand that this is a top secret research project, Amy. Very few people know what we were doing or who was here. And the scientists are used to working down here without any contact with the outside world for days on end if they have to.'

'But even so . . .'

'Got it!' The Doctor waved a sliver of moon rock in the air. 'Flash drive from one of the main computers – now we can find out what happened!'

Chris swallowed. 'But I just told you what happened.'

'I mean what *really* happened,' said the Doctor.

Amy looked curiously at the stone flash drive. It looked like an ordinary memory stick – only grey. 'How are you going to use that? It won't work if it's turned to stone.'

'Oh, I know a few tricks – and I've always got this.' He produced his sonic screwdriver in the other hand. 'And your mobile phone, please.'

Amy sighed and handed over her phone. The Doctor sat cross-legged on the floor and got to work, opening up Amy's phone first of all and then using the sonic screwdriver on the memory stick. 'It's just a case of finding the right data transference code between the flash drive and the phone . . .'

'But how can the flash drive still work if it's been turned to stone?' wondered Chris.

'All memory sticks use silicon microchip technology,' explained the Doctor. 'Silicon is a kind of rock. Now if I can create an interface between the chip and the display on the mobile . . .'

The sonic screwdriver hummed busily and the green light reflected from the Doctor's face in the darkness.

Amy wandered around the gloomy lab. There was just enough light coming from the corridor outside to see her way around. She stepped over rocky cables and around stone computer banks, exploring the strange machinery at the centre of the chamber. 'Is it safe to touch this, Doctor?'

'Oh yes, perfectly,' the Doctor replied without looking up from his work. 'The moon stone in here is all utterly inactive. It only appears to be the mobile Rock Men that have the ability to transform. Huh. There's a thought.'

'What?'

The Doctor concentrated on his task. 'What? Oh, nothing. Like I said – just a thought. Let me carry on thinking it for a second . . .'

Amy let her hand touch the stone machine, her fingers gliding over the smooth, cool surface as she walked around it. It was very dark on the other side, opposite the entrance. She held out her hand in front of her, unsure what was ahead. Then she touched a lumpy, rough shape that definitely wasn't a machine.

A startled gasp escaped from her lips as she realised what was in front of her.

Towering over her in the darkness was a dark, humanoid silhouette – carved from solid moon rock.

The Rock Man.

Chapter 20

The Heart of Stone

The Rock Man glowered at her with sightless eyes. It was utterly still.

'What is it?' asked the Doctor, joining her quickly. He had been alerted by her sharp cry of shock. 'Ah. The Rock Man.' The Doctor scanned it quickly. 'Dormant – luckily for us.'

Amy backed carefully away from the massive figure. 'It's not like the others. You can tell the others were once people – scientists. But this is just all lumpy and . . .'

'Not quite alien,' finished the Doctor. 'It's something else entirely. Not human, not alien and not ordinary moon rock. And I think I know why.'

He held up Amy's mobile. The screen was scrolling through a huge amount of information.

'I hope you're not online,' Amy joked. 'That'll cost me a fortune.'

'No, this is information I've downloaded from the flash drive. Chris said they were researching into the effect of UV light on the electrostatic fields surrounding moon rock. That in itself wouldn't trigger all this . . .' The Doctor gestured around the stone lab, '. . . and it wouldn't account for our rocky friend here. There had to be something else – something the scientists hadn't bargained for.'

'And you've found it?'

'Yes – alien bacteria.'

'Ew.'

The Doctor's fingers wiggled around in the air, full of enthusiasm for his subject. 'Bacteria! Brought back from the moon in the rock samples. Not in every piece – maybe just one. But it's very unusual bacteria – it's 3.9 billion year-old bacteria, the remains of an ancient, extinct civilisation. It probably arrived on the moon in its infancy, on a meteorite –' the Doctor pounded a fist into his other hand to demonstrate the impact, '*boom*! And it's been dormant ever since – trapped in the freezing dark on the airless surface of the moon. Some bacteria can live for decades – centuries even – and space-travelling bacteria even longer. Has to, if there's to be any chance of survival. And that's what this is all about – *survival.*'

'But now it's been brought to Earth from the moon,' Amy said, trying to follow the Doctor's train of thought.

'Yes, the *Apollo* astronauts must have picked up a piece of rock infected with this dormant space bacteria. It's been on Earth for years now – until suddenly the scientists here got hold of the rock and started bombarding it with ultraviolet light.' The Doctor's eyes lit up with excitement. 'And *bingo!*'

'The bacteria wakes up?'

'The bacteria wakes up!' The Doctor's expression hardened in the gloom. 'And it gets to work – controlling the electrostatic field contained in the moon rock, absorbing the UV rays and building itself a new body based on the first animal organism it's come into contact with in nearly four billion years.'

Amy's eyes widened. 'Human beings.'

'And so we have our lumpy Rock Man friend here.' The Doctor tapped the figure on the chest.

'But why change everything else into moon rock?'

'The bacteria is wild, uncontrollable. It's triggering molecular change at a fantastic, uncontrollable rate – trying to recreate an environment in which it feels at home.'

'So where's home?'

'Well, where's it been living for the past few billion years?'

'The moon.'

'Exactly. Good enough to call home now, I'd say.' The Doctor's deep-set eyes disappeared beneath a frown. 'But there's one question that remains.'

'Just one?'

'What on Earth does it want with Ralph Conway's farm?'

'I think I know the answer to that,' said Chris. It was the first time he'd spoken for some time. He was leaning against the doorway, partly silhouetted by the light outside.

'Yes,' said the Doctor. 'I should think you do.'

'The creature was after this,' Chris said. His voice sounded dull, as if he'd given up.

In his hand was a strangely shaped lump of grey rock.

'A piece of moon stone?' Amy queried.

Chris threw it to Amy. She caught it and then turned the rock around in her hands, angling it towards the light. 'It's shaped like a heart,' she said.

'Is this the original rock?' wondered the Doctor. He stepped closer and scanned the stone with his sonic screwdriver. The green light illuminated the grainy surface.

'Sample 247,' Chris said quietly. 'The Heart of Stone.'

'Figures,' said Amy.

'That's what we nicknamed it anyway. It must have contained the space bacteria you mentioned, Doctor.'

Amy gulped. 'Is it OK to handle it, then?'

'Probably,' said the Doctor. 'The meteorite was only activated by UV light, remember. And it's done its work already. Helped make Rocky here come to life.'

The Doctor gestured towards the motionless Rock Man.

And as he did so, the Rock Man suddenly grabbed the Heart of Stone right out of Amy's hand.

Chapter 21

The Statue Wakes

'Rory,' Jess called from the kitchen. 'Come and look at this!'

Rory, alerted by the note of anxiety in Jess's voice, came at a run. 'What's up?'

'I thought I saw him move.' Jess pointed out of the kitchen window at her father.

Ralph Conway still stood by the Land Rover, bound to the vehicle by chains and washing line. He didn't appear to have moved an inch.

'It was probably your imagination,' he told her gently.

'It wasn't my imagination at all,' Jess protested.

'A shadow, then – maybe a bird flew overhead and you saw the shadow crossing.'

She shook her head. 'No, Rory. I definitely saw him move!'

And then she pushed past him and ran out of the kitchen, heading across the yard to where her father stood like a statue.

Rory sighed and followed her out.

Jess came to a halt by the Land Rover and circled it. She stood in front of her father and looked up into his stone cold face. The eyes were open but unseeing. His hands were stiff where they gripped the chains.

Rory caught her up. 'It may even have been the sun – you know, the shadows changing as it moves.'

Jess shot him a look that said, *'Don't be stupid.'*

Rory had been on the receiving end of enough looks like that from Amy to recognise it easily.

'Negative electrostatics – that's what the Doctor said,' Rory pointed out. He wasn't completely sure what it meant but he could have a good guess. 'In other words, he can't move. The ultraviolet rays from the sun–'

'Oh, shush, Rory – use your eyes!'

Jess was holding her hand up towards her father's rigid face.

Rory immediately grabbed her wrist. 'Don't touch him –!'

But then he stopped.

Because he'd seen something moving on Ralph Conway's stone face.

The eyelids were starting to close. With a tiny, thin scraping noise, his eyes blinked. Once. Twice.

'Get back,' Rory said, pulling Jess away.

But she yanked herself free and ran back to her father. 'Dad!'

Ralph's stone head twisted around to look at her. Every movement was accompanied by the sound of scraping rock.

'We should get away,' Rory insisted. His heart was beating faster. Where was the Doctor when you really needed him? Swanning around in a flash sports car, that's where!

Ralph Conway flexed his shoulders and turned to face his daughter. The stone eyes seemed to find her, but how he could see was anyone's guess. His lips parted, slowly, painfully, and Rory winced at the sound they made.

Ralph pulled at the chains that held him, shifting them, gripping them in his stone hands until each link was transformed with a dull crack into moon stone and snapped.

The chain fell away in ruins and the washing line parted, breaking into tiny, brittle pieces.

'Move,' said Rory, gripping Jess's hand and pulling her towards the farmhouse.

'No, wait . . .'

But Ralph had started to follow them with slow, plodding footsteps.

Rory half dragged Jess into the farmhouse. Once inside the kitchen he turned to close and lock the door – only to find that the door was already missing, along with part of the frame.

'Uh, we have a problem developing . . .' Rory muttered, as Ralph approached the door.

'What's he going to do?' asked Jess.

Rory snapped around, searching for something to use to defend themselves. He could hear the dull *scrape* . . . *scrape* . . . *scrape* of the man's approach behind him.

And then suddenly Ralph stood in the remains of the doorway.

Rory picked up the last remaining kitchen chair and faced Ralph like a lion tamer, holding the chair legs out towards him.

'Don't come any closer!' Rory told him, but his voice came out like a tight little squeak.

Ralph stepped into the kitchen.

'Oh, crumbs!' Rory backed away, keeping the chair up. 'Stay behind me, Jess.'

The stone man started walking towards them.

Chapter 22

Run!

'Amy!' shouted the Doctor. Amy staggered backwards, horrified. The Rock Man lurched out of the shadows, its fist closed tight around the Heart of Stone.

'Not good!' yelled the Doctor, grabbing hold of Amy and helping her away. 'Not at all good . . .'

They tripped over a stone cable and crashed to the floor. The Rock Man stomped towards them.

'Up!' shouted the Doctor, hauling Amy to her feet.

They pelted across the room, dodging past moon rock workstations and under dangling stone power lines.

'This way!' cried Chris, calling them across the chamber as the Rock Man charged.

It crashed through a databank, hurling the thing to one side – where it smashed into fragments.

The Doctor, Amy and Chris ran, as moon rock shrapnel scattered across the floor.

'We've got to stop it,' the Doctor said, scrambling over a stone power converter. He helped the others climb over.

'Can't we just get out of here?' Chris asked.

'And let it come after us?'

Amy looked back to where the ugly shape of the creature loomed in the darkness. It didn't seem to care where it went or what it smashed to get to them. Clouds of grey moon dust were beginning to fill the chamber.

'What made it come alive again?' she asked the Doctor. 'I thought it was only ultraviolet light – sunshine.'

'The bacteria must be adapting,' replied the Doctor. 'The meteorite is learning to use any kind of energy source – including the sonic screwdriver. Look out!'

The Rock Man smashed the power converter and strode through the debris.

The Doctor, Amy and Chris headed further into the depths of the secret lab – and further into the darkness.

The Doctor used the sonic screwdriver to light their way – the equipment here was packed closer together, linked by hundreds of wires and cables and junction boxes. It was like climbing through a stone jungle in the dark. The torchlight crept over the strange grey shapes as they picked their way through.

The Rock Man charged after them. It paused on the edge of the stone jungle, the dim light reflecting from its grey face. The deep holes that served as eyes were as black as night as they peered into the shadows.

The Doctor, Amy and Chris crouched behind a databank, hardly daring to breathe.

The Rock Man moved slowly forward, its heavy feet dragging across the stone floor with a harsh scraping noise.

The three of them remained absolutely still.

And suddenly the Rock Man heaved aside the databank, splintering the moon rock into a thousand dusty pieces, revealing the Doctor and his friends in an instant.

Amy screamed as she dived out of the way. The Doctor was right behind her, pulling Chris after him.

The Rock Man's massive hand swept down, crunching into the floor where the three of them had been a second before.

With a snarl of savage anger, the Rock Man charged after them. It thrashed its way through the power lines. The stone girders that helped support the central machinery crumbled.

There was a deep groan from above.

The Doctor's head snapped up and he shone his torch towards the ceiling. The huge stone ramparts that secured the machine stretched up into the shadows. Dust was falling like rain.

'It's going to destroy this place,' he realised.

Chris was appalled. 'It cost millions to put this lot together!'

'All a bit useless if it's made out of stone, though,' the Doctor pointed out.

There was a loud creak and fragments of rocks fell from above, scattering down through the machinery and onto the floor.

'We have to get out of here,' Amy said.

The Rock Man had almost caught them up. It shoved aside more computer workstations, leaving a trail of chaos.

The Doctor glanced up again. Then he turned to Amy and Chris. 'Head for the door – I'll meet you outside.'

'We can't leave you,' Amy protested.

'Just do as I say!'

Chris grabbed Amy's hand. 'Come on, Amy!'

The Doctor was already climbing onto the nearest workstation. From there he clambered across to a taller piece of machinery festooned with cables that snaked up into the branches of the central complex.

With a last, despairing look, Amy followed Chris, heading towards the exit. She had a horrible feeling she knew what the Doctor was planning.

The Rock Man saw Amy and Chris run – but the Doctor was still nearer. Craning its thick neck, the creature turned its pitiless black eyes up towards him.

The Doctor was hanging on to one of the support struts, leaning unsteadily out over the laboratory.

Letting go with one hand, the Doctor held his sonic screwdriver out at arm's length. He pointed it straight up into the shadows and activated it.

The tip glowed a fierce green and a shrill whine filled the chamber.

Something cracked like a gunshot in the darkness. The Doctor pointed the screwdriver in another direction and repeated the process. There was another huge crack – followed by a series of splintering noises. Dust cascaded from the ceiling.

Amy stopped at the doorway and looked up. The Doctor adjusted his aim again, and more dust rained down as a series of loud cracks echoed through the lab.

Everything started to shake.

'What's he doing?' Chris wondered.

'Using the sonic to vibrate the moon rock and crack it,' Amy said. 'He's going to bring this whole place down!'

The Doctor was climbing slowly down – he had to go carefully because the whole structure was shaking. He had the sonic screwdriver gripped between his teeth.

The Rock Man lumbered towards him, splitting a monitor bank in two with a scraping growl. Its hands reached out to grab the Doctor – but he was too quick for the creature.

He slipped down the last couple of metres, landed awkwardly and fell. The Rock Man's hands closed on dusty air.

The Doctor rolled along the floor, sprang to his feet and dodged past the creature. As he ran he held the sonic screwdriver out behind him and activated it.

A piercing whine shot through the air. The Doctor raised his arm, directing the sonic screwdriver straight up.

There was an almighty, splintering crack from above.

A huge piece of machinery dislodged from the ceiling and fell down, crashing into the rest of the apparatus below. Dust billowed out from the wreckage.

The Rock Man started after the Doctor.

The Doctor skidded to a stop by the door where

Amy and Chris were waiting.

'When I say run,' panted the Doctor, 'run!'

They took one last look at the lab. The Rock Man roared and headed straight for them – and then the entire chamber shook as if gripped by an earthquake and the whole thing collapsed.

The central machinery cracked and fell into pieces, crashing down with a terrible noise. Sections of the ceiling tumbled after it, dragged down as the support legs gave way. Tons of moon rock crashed to the floor and a huge, thick cloud of choking dust rolled up.

The Doctor, Amy and Chris waited for the last pieces to fall. The entire lab had been destroyed – there was nothing left now but a pile of rubble.

'Do you think that thing is dead now?' asked Chris.

'It was never truly alive – not in the way you mean,' said the Doctor sadly.

'But it's done for, isn't it?'

'I doubt anything could survive that,' said Amy.

The Doctor peered at the huge mound of grey waste. 'It must have been crushed,' he said. 'But look . . .'

Sticking out from the base of the wreckage, there was a rocky hand.

It still gripped the Heart of Stone.

The Doctor, covering his nose and mouth with a hanky so that he didn't breathe in the moon dust, crept back to the hand. He bent down and gently worked the stone loose.

'Why do you want that?' Amy asked.

'This rock is what started it all, remember,' said the Doctor. 'We don't want to leave it in the wrong hands.'

He wrapped the stone in his handkerchief and put it in a pocket. 'Come on – let's go.'

Pieces of moon rock continued to fall, clattering down through the debris. Dust swirled.

And, faintly, the Rock Man's fingers began to move . . .

Chapter 23

Explanations

Rory tried to position himself in front of Jess. He wasn't sure this was a very good idea, but it felt like the kind of thing he should do.

The Rock Man – in the shape of Ralph Conway – continued to approach.

And then Jess stepped past Rory and held out her hands to her father.

'Dad,' she said. 'It's me – stop.'

And, remarkably, Ralph Conway did stop.

'Don't get any closer,' hissed Rory. He didn't want to see Jess turned to stone as well.

But a very strange thing was happening. Jess was inching closer to the stone figure before her. And he was staying absolutely still.

'Be careful,' Rory insisted.

'I think it's OK,' Jess whispered. 'Really, I do . . .'

She took another step.

Ralph Conway's head dipped slightly lower, as if he was about to say something.

'Dad?' Jess said gently.

Ralph's grey lips parted slightly and a horrible scraping sound emerged. It looked like he was trying to speak, but it was causing him terrible pain.

'It's all right,' Jess said. 'Don't try to talk. I understand.'

'You do?' said Rory.

'He doesn't want to hurt us,' Jess said. 'Look at him. He's terrified.'

'Look at *me*,' said Rory. 'I'm terrified too.'

Ralph fell silent. He remained completely still.

Encouraged, Rory came a little closer. Every line in Conway's face, every tiny bit of stubble and mark on his skin, was perfectly captured in stone. It was astonishing – more than a work of art, in fact. There was no man-made sculpture in the world like this.

'We'll get you back, Dad,' Jess said softly. She turned to Rory. 'Won't we?'

'Yeah, of course.' But Rory couldn't for the life of him see how.

There was an abrupt knock at the door – or rather the door frame. Rory and Jess had hardly turned their heads before Mr Hoggett strode uninvited into the farmhouse.

'Door was open,' he explained snootily. 'In fact, the door was missing. Like half the rest of this dump. It's in a state of collapse, you know.'

'I thought we'd seen the last of you, Mr Hoggett,' said Jess.

'The only way you'll see the last of me, my dear girl, is when you agree to sell this hopeless excuse for a farm.' Hoggett smiled wolfishly.

Then something else caught his attention. Hoggett's face darkened as he saw Ralph Conway.

'I can't believe you brought that awful thing inside,' he said. 'But then I suppose it's better than having it on display outside. Always thought Conway had too high an opinion of himself – but a *statue*, for goodness' sake!'

The statue's head turned slowly and glared at Hoggett.

Hoggett practically choked.

Jess and Rory watched him turn pale, then red and then almost black with fury.

'What . . .' Hoggett spluttered, 'what on Earth is this meant to be? Some kind of joke?'

'Well,' began Rory, and then stopped. He couldn't think of anything to say.

'Explain!' thundered Hoggett.

'It's really very simple,' said the Doctor, sweeping into the room unannounced.

Every head snapped around to look at him and Amy. Every head except Ralph Conway's, which turned slowly with a harsh grinding noise.

Chris Jenkins appeared in the door frame behind Amy.

'Chris!' exclaimed Jess, her voice full of shock and delight – and a hint of uncertainty. 'Chris? Are you all right?'

'I'm not sure,' he replied.

Hoggett continued to splutter with indignant anger. 'What's going on? Who are these people? What's happening?'

'Hello,' said the Doctor, waving his fingers briefly at the irritated man. 'I'm the Doctor, this is Amy, that is Chris – Jess's fiancé – and that is Rory – Amy's husband – I know, it's beginning to get confusing, but don't worry, all will become very clear in a moment.' The Doctor clapped his hands together with some satisfaction.

Hoggett pointed a trembling finger at Ralph Conway. 'And this?'

'This is Ralph Conway, Jess's father,' the Doctor explained patiently.

Hoggett's finger continued to tremble, but it was

impossible to tell whether this was due to fear or anger.
'I know *who* it is . . .' he said through gritted teeth.

'Ah,' realised the Doctor. 'You're wondering why
he appears to be made of stone.'

'But –'

'That's because he is, in fact, made of stone.'

'But –'

'And not just any old stone,' the Doctor continued
brightly. 'But *moon* stone. That's rather extraordinary,
don't you think?'

'But –'

The Doctor let out an exasperated sigh. 'But what?'

'But it *moved*!'

'Ah, yes,' the Doctor nodded slowly. 'That is the
other extraordinary thing. Isn't it wonderful that one
day could be so full of so many extraordinary things?
They're the days I love best, to be honest.'

Hoggett was seething. 'Will someone please
explain *exactly* what is going on here?'

There was silence as everyone looked at the Doctor.

'That would be me, then,' said the Doctor. 'Well,
as I said, it's really quite simple. It started when a
meteorite crashed into the surface of this planet's
moon nearly four billion years ago. Lovely big crater,
tiny little something left at the centre. An alien
something. Carrying alien bacteria. Special alien

bacteria that lay on the cold, airless surface of the moon until an unsuspecting astronaut from the last *Apollo* mission collected it as part of a sample of moon rocks to bring back to Earth for study. All clear so far?'

Silence.

'Good, I'll carry on. We're getting to the good bit! Not all the moon rock samples were tested straight away. Some were, some were given away as presents to foreign governments and some were kept for display. Some were held back for further investigation. And some – including the one carrying our special alien bacteria – were sent for analysis by Chris and his friends here at the Research Institute.'

Chris gave a little wave.

'Chris and his friends bombarded the moon rocks with ultraviolet light – and the special alien bacteria reacted. This is what it had been waiting 3.9 billion years for. So, it reacted pretty quickly, because, let's face it, it had been waiting for a long, long time and was getting pretty impatient. And it used its own unique and special talent: to change whatever it touched into something that it could use as a body.'

'Change?' said Hoggett.

'Molecular reconfiguration,' nodded the Doctor. He wiggled his fingers together in a complicated pattern as he spoke. 'Transforming metal, plastic, wood, skin, bone, *anything* at all, into moon rock.'

'And your point about the moon bacteria is?' prompted Jess.

'It's natural. It can't help what it does. You humans always wanted to fly, and it took you ages to *make* gliders and wings and engines and build something you could fly *in*. But the birds and the bees have been doing it since forever. *Naturally.* They can't help it. And that's just like the moon bacteria. It can't help changing things.'

The Doctor turned in a slow circle, ensuring everyone was still listening. Hoggett's mouth was hanging open, and the Doctor reached out and gently closed it.

'The bacteria copied the first real life form it discovered, fashioning a humanoid body for itself.'

'The Rock Man,' said Amy.

The Doctor nodded thoughtfully. His dark eyes glowered from beneath his heavy brow. 'And then. Then it went looking for something.'

Chapter 24
Chris's Secret

'Looking for what?' asked Rory. 'Sorry, I'm not following this at all.'

The Doctor smiled. 'It went looking for a particular rock: the lunar sample that had started it all. The source of the bacteria.'

'Which was where?' asked Jess.

'Here,' answered the Doctor. 'In the farmhouse.'

'But – how?'

'Ask Chris.'

Jess turned to Chris with a puzzled frown. 'Chris?'

Chris looked uncomfortable. 'I . . . brought it here. From the research centre. I'm sorry, I really didn't know what I was doing. But I knew the rock was trouble. I'd seen the effect it had produced at the research centre, turning everything and everyone I knew into moon stone. I was scared. But I knew I had to get the rock away from the centre, in case it happened again. So I hid it here.'

'You never told me.'

'I didn't want to frighten you. I was trying to think of a way to deal with everything. I'd only just got your Dad to accept me – almost, anyway – and I didn't want anything to risk that.'

Jess looked at her father, still turned to stone. 'I think you risked *everything*.'

'Possibly,' the Doctor agreed. 'But Chris really didn't know what he was dealing with. And he couldn't have known that the Rock Man would come looking for the stone – which, incidentally, I have here in my pocket.'

He took the heart-shaped lump of rock from his jacket pocket.

'You mean that's what brought the Rock Man to the farm?' asked Jess.

'Yes. He arrived in the middle of the night, knocked down your wall – accidentally changing it into moon rock – blundered around a bit and then got scared off by your father.'

'I came straight away,' Chris continued. 'I wanted to take the Heart of Stone back – or at least, away from here.'

'Heart of Stone?' queried Rory.

The Doctor held up the rock. 'Yeah, looks a bit like a human heart. Complete coincidence. In fact, it doesn't really look like that at all.'

He produced the sonic screwdriver in his other hand and pointed it at the rock. The tip shone green and a shrill noise filled the room. Suddenly, the rock cracked and disintegrated in a puff of grey dust that trickled through the Doctor's fingers.

The Doctor snapped the sonic screwdriver off. Left in his other hand was something a little smaller than the original rock – something smooth, spherical and black. It was about the size of a tennis ball, but glossy, like a hugely magnified droplet of oil.

'What is it?' asked Rory, his eyes wide.

'This is the original meteorite that struck the moon all those millennia ago.' The Doctor held the sphere out for them to see. 'It's from another galaxy altogether. Here, catch.'

The Doctor tossed the ball casually to Mr Hoggett, who caught it instinctively. He looked at the ball and then at the Doctor, opening and closing his mouth but not making a sound.

The Doctor smiled. 'The moon rock was just the outer layer, thickening around that ball over billions of years.'

'I left the Heart of Stone here, hoping to hide it

until I worked out what to do,' said Chris. He looked miserably at Jess. 'I'm sorry.'

'The Rock Man came back the next night, while you were here,' Jess said. 'You knew what it was and why it was here. And yet you ran away.'

Chris looked shamefaced, but the Doctor said, 'Actually, Chris saved us all last night, Jess. He took the meteorite away with him, knowing the Rock Man would follow him – and leave you alone.'

'But not before the Rock Man had smashed the place to bits and done *that* to my dad!' Jess pointed at her father, who stood like a statue in the middle of the room.

'And that's where the good news comes in,' said the Doctor brightly. 'I'm pretty sure we can change your dad back to normal.'

Jess stifled a sob. 'How?'

'Using the meteorite.' The Doctor plucked the black sphere out of Mr Hoggett's hands. 'The change is highly unstable – it's constantly on the edge of being permanent. But that means it's also right on the edge of being temporary. If I can tap into the molecular code contained in this meteorite and reverse it, everything should turn out hunky-dory.'

'Did you really just say "hunky-dory"?' laughed Amy.

The Doctor winced. 'It won't happen again, I promise.'

Jess had turned to Chris, wiping away a tear. 'Is it true? Can he get Dad back to normal?'

Chris nodded. 'If the Doctor says he can, then I believe him. And so should you.'

'It may take a few minutes to calculate the code,' said the Doctor. He cleared a space on the kitchen table and sat down. 'It's probably some kind of binary-electron code – something natural and basic . . .' He fished in his pocket and produced a jeweller's eyeglass, which he screwed into place so that he could examine the meteorite in minute detail.

Chris took Jess by the hand. 'Do you forgive me, Jess? I'm sorry for the trouble I've caused.'

'Why didn't you tell me what was going on in the first place?'

'I didn't think you'd believe me. And worse than that – I thought you might call the engagement off. Or your dad would.'

Jess touched his cheek tenderly. 'I just wanted you back, Chris, that's all.'

At this point the Doctor looked up from his work. 'You know, this is a very difficult job and requires total concentration. A little quiet would help. You can save the soppy stuff for later.'

Jess smiled and squeezed Chris's hand. 'Anything you say, Doctor.'

'Good.' The Doctor clicked open his sonic screwdriver. 'Now, complete silence, please.'

His only answer was a terrific crash from the remains of the kitchen doorway – and the sight of the Rock Man looming through the gap, grey hands outstretched . . .

Chapter 25

The Doctor Changes

'Oh, not you again,' complained the Doctor. 'What the dickens is *that*?' roared Mr Hoggett as the Rock Man stepped into the farmhouse.

Everyone backed away quickly – everyone except the Doctor, who jumped to his feet and walked swiftly towards the creature, his sonic screwdriver at the ready.

'Hello . . .' he began.

The Rock Man gave a gravelly snarl.

'I'm so glad you survived the – er – rockfall,' continued the Doctor. 'And I thought you'd probably come after me. Or rather – this.'

In his other hand he held up the glossy black sphere.

'I've just been having a bit of a tinker,' the Doctor

confessed. 'You know, trying to see what makes it tick and how I might use it to return poor Mr Conway back to his usual self . . .'

The Doctor pointed at Ralph Conway.

The Rock Man's dark eye-pits turned towards the stone farmer. Its jaws scraped together as it seemed to consider.

'You see, we have a communication problem here,' the Doctor went on. 'I can't understand a word you're saying. My guess is that your species has been mutated so far from its original form that it's *beyond* alien. It's something completely new and unique.'

The Rock Man growled.

The Doctor regarded it sadly. 'It's not even like you're a long, long way from home. You don't even *have* a home.'

The Rock Man growled again, and the noise was like a paving slab being dragged over concrete.

'What can I do to help?' the Doctor asked.

Everyone watched in amazement as the Doctor stood calmly before the towering grey creature, looking directly into the deep, dark pits where its eyes should be.

He was close enough for the creature to reach out and crush him – or turn him to stone.

And then the Rock Man did reach out.

And pointed a stubby, rocky finger at the Doctor's own hand.

The hand that held the meteorite ball.

'Yes,' the Doctor whispered. 'I think I understand.' He held the ball up slowly. 'This is your home?'

The Rock Man leaned forward and, very carefully, touched the ball.

It was impossible to tell exactly what happened in that moment.

There was no flash of light, no spark, no crackle or rumble of thunder.

But somehow, something – everything – changed in that moment. It was as if a connection had been made with something strange and mysterious – a connection between the Rock Man and the Doctor.

The Doctor stiffened – literally.

The hand that held the meteorite turned rigid, pale.

And then grey, like moon rock.

'Doctor!' gasped Amy.

The sleeve of the Doctor's tweed jacket changed to grey, the elbow patch stiffened and turned to stone.

'Oh, my goodness,' breathed Jess. 'No, please, no – not again . . .'

The Doctor turned his head to look at the others. His deep eyes blazed with fierce intent, the incredible mind behind them burning with the effort of speaking.

'Don't do anything – don't do anything at all,' he said gruffly.

And then his eyes turned solid.

The dreadful greyness had seeped up his neck and turned his face into a pallid, eerie stone. His hair whitened like that of an old man and stiffened, the heavy fringe apparently carved from solid rock.

In less than a few seconds, the Doctor had been completely transformed. He stood like a statue, holding the meteorite ball, with the Rock Man still touching it.

Amy held Rory tightly and screamed, '*Doctor*!'

Chapter 26
Athrocite

The Doctor had been transformed entirely into moon rock.

His head turned slowly towards his friends with a terrible grinding noise. And then his grey lips parted in a smile.

'It's all right,' he said. His voice sounded dry and gravelly, completely unlike normal. It was a sound that made the hairs on Rory's neck stand up and he felt Amy's body wilt next to him.

And yet . . .

And yet the Doctor was smiling – sort of.

It wasn't easy to tell with his features turned to stone, but the lips were definitely smiling, even if there was a vague look of pain in his flat, grey eyes.

'It's OK,' he rumbled again. 'I'm fine. Really.'

He raised his arms, spreading the fingers of his rock-like hands.

'Well, not exactly *fine*,' he ground on, 'not fine in the *normal* sense . . .'

He stepped slowly forward, arms held awkwardly as if trying to maintain his balance in a body that must have felt so strange and heavy. His grey boots clumped across the carpet as he approached Amy and Rory.

'I mean – look at me!' The stone Doctor examined his own hand closely. 'I'm made of moon rock! Moon rock moving using negative electrostatic energy. Isn't that *amazing*?'

'It is . . . amazing,' Rory agreed. But he looked very uncertain.

'Amazing,' Amy echoed. 'But not what we expected. Or wanted.'

'It's all right,' the Doctor insisted.

He was trying to sound reassuring, but the harsh, scraping tones sounded totally alien coming from the Doctor.

'I knew this would happen,' the Doctor told them. 'Sort of. Well, more of a guess, really.'

'What on Earth have you done?' Amy finally blurted, unable to stop herself. She put her hands up to her face, blinking away tears.

'Don't get upset,' urged the Doctor.

He reached out for Amy but she recoiled. 'Don't touch me! I don't want to be turned to stone!'

But the Doctor had reached a little too far – and started to topple over. He moved quickly, for someone made out of rock, and regained his balance. 'Whoa! Gotta be careful here. One slip and crack! I'll go all to pieces.'

'Doctor,' said Jess. 'What have you done?'

The Doctor turned slowly and carefully to face Jess. 'Only the most incredible and amazing thing I've done so far today. And I try to do something like that almost every day. I've been turned to stone.'

'We can see that.'

'So, now I know what it's like to be like your dad. Or the Rock Man here.' The Doctor pointed to the towering creature behind him.

The Rock Man was simply watching the Doctor through its shadowy eyes, as if wondering what he might do next.

'But Dad can't move or speak – at least, not properly.'

'That's because he's only human,' replied the Doctor. 'I'm something else. And so is our friend here. We can use the negative electrostatic energy to move more easily. Well, a bit more easily. And that's not all.'

The Doctor turned and said something to the Rock Man. But not in English, or any kind of language anyone else in the room had ever heard. It sounded more like one slab of concrete being pulled across another.

And the Rock Man replied in kind.

'Can you two understand each other?' asked Amy.

The Doctor nodded slowly. 'Absolutely. Athrocite here can finally communicate. And I can only understand him because I now share the same molecular structure. It's a complicated and totally unique way to talk.' The Doctor's stone hand reached up to touch his stone throat. 'Plays hell with the vocal chords, mind you. Especially when they're made entirely of stone.'

'So, what's he saying?' Amy wanted to know.

'And did you just call him by his *name*?' Rory asked.

'Yes. I'm calling him Athrocite. I don't know if it's his actual name or the name of his original species. But it seems nicer than Rock Man.'

'But what's he actually saying?' Amy insisted.

The Doctor bit his stone lip. 'What he's saying is this: "How can I get away from this dreadful place?"'

There was an uncomfortable silence.

'Or words to that effect,' the Doctor added

nervously. 'Place . . . planet . . . it's difficult to be certain. And it loses a little in translation.'

Athrocite snarled something and the Doctor nodded. 'Yes, yes, I'm trying to explain . . . Keep your hair on. Not that you've actually got any.'

'For Heaven's sake,' snarled Mr Hoggett, his face redder than ever. 'No one invited him here. Fellow's some kind of monster if you ask me.'

'I didn't,' said the Doctor pointedly.

'Or is this just some kind of stupid practical joke?' Hoggett demanded to know. His lips twisted into a sneer of contempt. 'You look like a student.'

'It's not a joke,' said the Doctor. 'And I'm not a student.'

'Because it's not in the least bit funny,' Hoggett continued.

Athrocite rumbled something else.

'Athrocite says he never meant to come here,' the Doctor translated. He took the ball from Athrocite's hand. 'His distant ancestors arrived on the moon in this meteorite. Scientists experimented on the meteorite and it formed a new kind of life, roughly based on a human being. In other words – Athrocite was born. So far, so good. But anything he touched was transformed into the same material. The research lab, the scientists, anything at all. Disastrous. And it won't stop there. The process is highly unstable – there's no way to control it, and if we don't find a way to stop it . . .'

'What will happen, Doctor?' asked Amy.

The Doctor's tone was deadly serious. 'It won't stop – ever. It'll keep on going, transforming, until everything and everyone and everywhere is made of moon rock.'

Chapter 27

Shut Up, Hoggett

'Everything?' said Amy. 'We have to find a way to stop it – to get Athrocite away from here. Away from the planet.'

But Athrocite was growing impatient – a dark maw opened in his craggy face, releasing a grating howl. He seemed to loom taller in the room and the others backed quickly away.

'Please,' the Doctor pleaded with the Rock Man. 'You must understand – I'm doing my best to help you. But time is running out and I have to explain . . .'

Athrocite swept angrily at the air and the Doctor jerked backwards, raising his hands. 'Steady!'

The creature roared and stretched out, past the Doctor's head, snatching at Rory.

Rory darted backwards, Amy holding onto him all the time. 'What does it want?'

'The meteorite,' said the Doctor.

And then he turned back to Athrocite. 'Calm down – I want to help but you must be patient!'

Athrocite snarled again and stepped towards Rory.

'Should I hand it back?' Rory asked, holding the meteorite close to his chest as he looked uncertainly at the Doctor.

'Not yet.' The Doctor pointed the sonic screwdriver at the Rock Man. 'I'll use this if I have to, Athrocite!'

The creature turned its baleful, empty eyes on the Doctor.

The Doctor triggered the sonic screwdriver – but nothing happened.

Like the Doctor, the sonic screwdriver was now made entirely of moon rock.

'There's plenty more where that came from,' warned the Doctor helplessly.

'What the Devil are you trying to do?' asked Hoggett. 'It's had absolutely no effect!'

The Doctor glared at him. 'I can see *that*,' he hissed. 'I had hoped to freeze him for a second or two, but . . .'

Athrocite glowered at the Doctor, eyeing the sonic screwdriver with suspicion.

'Get on with it, then!' seethed Hoggett. 'Drive him

away! Keep prodding him with that thing and it'll drive him away!'

The Doctor tried to run a hand through his hair in exasperation, only to find his hair was all made of stone as well as the sonic screwdriver and his fingers only scraped noisily across his head. His grey eyes glared at Hoggett.

'You just don't get it, do you?' the Doctor shouted. 'This creature is *totally* unique. And frightened. That makes him dangerous – he's massively powerful, but he's struggling to contain it. What if he decides he's had enough? Or panics? He could turn everything and everyone here to moon stone in an instant. And then the farm. And the surrounding countryside. When will it stop? The rest of the country? The whole planet?'

The Doctor's voice was raised now and both Amy and Rory could see that he was under intense pressure to resolve the situation.

Athrocite kept watching the Doctor, and then Hoggett, and then the Doctor again as the argument went back and forth.

But Hoggett didn't seem to care – or understand. He rounded angrily on the Doctor, his face reddening. 'If you know so much about all this, why don't you just explain to the wretched thing that it's not welcome here?'

'Athrocite doesn't entirely trust me – or any human being,' the Doctor replied. 'And why would he? He's *completely* alien to your world – he's something entirely new, with origins in the dawn of time.' He turned and looked up at Athrocite, his tone softening. 'In fact, it's a privilege just to be standing here.'

Hoggett spluttered. 'A privilege? You don't know what you're blathering about, man!'

'Doctor,' interrupted Amy. 'What can we do? How can we help him?'

'I had hoped to persuade him to come with us in the TARDIS – to take him to another planet, somewhere in the Pron-Kalunka Galaxy where there are lots and lots of silicon-based life forms.'

Athrocite was growing impatient again, a long, low, scraping growl escaping from deep within his rocky torso.

The Doctor turned and spoke to him in his own language, and the two of them exchanged a number of strange, unearthly noises.

'Well?' asked Amy. 'Will he do it?'

'He wants to know what's wrong with *this* planet,' replied the Doctor.

'Nothing,' said Amy. 'Except that it's ours.'

'But Athrocite doesn't have a planet of his own, Amy. What's the difference?'

'I've had just about enough of this,' Hoggett erupted. 'The thing is made of rock. Why don't you just take a ruddy great sledgehammer to it?'

'*I'm* made of rock!' the Doctor objected. 'Do you want to take a sledgehammer to me too?'

'Yes!' Hoggett yelled. Then he turned to face Athrocite. 'I don't know who or what you are, because none of this makes the slightest bit of sense to me – but I do know this: you don't belong here, you're not wanted here, and you –'

Hoggett froze mid sentence.

His face stiffened.

He turned grey, greyer . . . and with a sharp cracking sound he turned to solid stone.

There was complete silence. Everyone simply stood and looked at him.

Ralph Conway had reached out and gripped Mr Hoggett's shoulder from behind. The effect of the touch had been instant – Hoggett had been transformed into moon rock.

'Dad!' said Jess, a hand to her mouth in shock.

'Thank goodness someone found a way to shut him up,' said the Doctor. 'What a very annoying man. Did anyone else think he was a very annoying man?'

Everyone else nodded immediately.

And then Rory said, 'Um, Doctor . . . Athrocite seems to have left.'

The Doctor snapped around. The Rock Man had vanished.

Chapter 28

Not a Second to Lose

'No!' cried the Doctor, rushing out of the farmhouse. 'No, no, no!'

Rory and Amy ran out after him, closely followed by Chris. 'Where did he go?'

'There!' The Doctor pointed.

Athrocite was stomping away across the yard.

'Come back!' the Doctor yelled.

Athrocite turned slowly around, eyes narrowed. A low growl scraped out of his mouth.

'Maybe that wasn't such a good idea,' said Amy.

The Doctor darted forward, slipped, nearly fell, scraping his hand along the brickwork of the wall.

'Be careful!' Chris told him. 'You're made of rock,

remember! If you fall and break –'

'Good point,' agreed the Doctor, regaining his balance.

'Athrocite looks *really* angry,' said Rory.

'Between him and Mr Hoggett, it's a wonder we're all still standing,' said Amy. 'I've never seen such bad tempers.'

'At least Athrocite has an excuse,' said the Doctor.

'True,' agreed Rory. 'But he doesn't have this.' He held up the meteorite ball.

The Doctor leapt over to him, regardless of the risk. 'Rory! That's brilliant! You've still got the meteorite!'

'It's what Athrocite wants, isn't it?'

'Definitely,' nodded the Doctor. 'Probably. Maybe. Let's hope so. Quickly – back inside the farmhouse.'

Back inside the kitchen, the Doctor took the meteorite ball and put it down on the table. 'This might be just what we need.'

'I thought you said Athrocite needs it?' said Amy.

'He does – the negative electrostatic field that allows him to move, and me and Ralph and Mr Hoggett here, is tied right into the energy field contained in this meteorite.' The Doctor stared at the glossy black ball, and Amy could tell, even though he was made of stone, that his fantastic mind was already coming up with a plan. 'It's my guess that the molecular reconfiguration is controlled by a similar field.'

'What do you mean?'

'I've been thinking about Athrocite and his ability to turn things into moon stone. Do you remember I said that the transformation was unstable, and therefore reversible?' The Doctor paced quickly around the kitchen. 'Well, that's true – but only up to a point. Because once enough Earth matter has been converted, then it will reach a tipping point.'

'Which means?'

The Doctor stopped. 'Which means that the transformation will start to spread faster and faster. And it will be unstoppable. And it will not be possible to reverse it.'

'The point of no return,' realised Chris.

'But that means it could take over . . . everywhere,' said Amy. 'And everything.'

'We have to stop it,' said the Doctor. 'And this meteorite is the key. We have to keep it away from Athrocite – as far away as possible.'

'But he'll follow it anywhere,' said Chris. 'He followed it all the way from the research centre to here.'

'I was thinking of taking it somewhat further away than that,' said the Doctor. He turned to Amy. 'Stay here with Chris and Jess – make sure no harm comes to Mr Conway or Mr Hoggett. And whatever you do, don't let Athrocite back in.'

Jess gaped at him, trying to imagine keeping the huge Rock Man from entering the farmhouse. 'What? How?'

'I don't know – you'll think of something.' The Doctor turned to Rory. 'Rory, I'm going to need your help. I can't move all that fast, so you'll have to take the meteorite.' He gave it to Rory. 'We'll go as a pair. On the count of three . . .'

'Hold on,' said Rory quickly. 'What are you talking about?'

'We need to get that meteorite on-board the TARDIS,' explained the Doctor, already heading for the door. 'And that means we've got to get past Athrocite first. Come on – there's not a second to lose!'

Chapter 29
To the TARDIS

They crept out into the farmyard, keeping low so that Athrocite couldn't easily spot them.

The Rock Man was still standing at the top end of the yard, surrounded by moon stone. He was deliberately touching more and more things – the barn, the engine shed, a tree – and transforming them into lunar rock.

'What's he doing?' whispered Rory.

'Turning everything he can get his hands on into moon rock,' replied the Doctor, as quietly as he could manage with his rasping rock-voice. 'He's trying to change everything – to reach the tipping point. Soon the effect will be unstoppable.'

'We'd best get a move on then.' Rory crept out from behind the Land Rover and motioned for the Doctor to follow him.

Together they moved slowly up the farmyard, towards the TARDIS.

But that also took them nearer to Athrocite.

'Hopefully he's too busy trying to create a new world to notice us,' said the Doctor as they paused by the edge of the barn.

They moved on, darting from cover to cover.

Then disaster struck.

The Doctor's stone foot hit the edge of a pile of logs balanced against the side of the shed. Athrocite had already turned the logs into moon stone – but they were still loose. The Doctor's boot dislodged one of the lowermost logs – and the rest came tumbling down with a loud clatter.

Athrocite lumbered around, alerted by the noise.

But that wasn't all. The Doctor's legs had got caught up in the rock fall and he sprawled his length on the ground. For a hearts-stopping moment he thought he was going to be smashed to pieces.

'Doctor!' Rory skidded to a halt, eyes wide. He watched Athrocite start towards the fallen Doctor.

Rory panicked, thinking the Doctor must surely have cracked.

But the Doctor, miraculously, had landed in a large patch of mud. He slithered to a stop and tried to get up, but it was impossible to get a grip on the slippery ground.

Athrocite stalked towards him with a triumphant growl.

'Go!' the Doctor shouted at Rory.

Athrocite turned to see Rory on the other side of the yard.

The distraction was just enough for the Doctor. He crawled through the mud and dragged himself carefully up, using the wall of the barn for support.

Rory looked uncertainly at the Doctor, and then at the Rock Man.

And ran.

Athrocite roared and turned back to face the Doctor. He growled again as the stone figure walked calmly towards him.

'There's no point in getting all cross about it,' said the Doctor. 'You had your chance.'

Athrocite roared, flailing at him with a craggy arm. If the blow had connected, the Doctor would have been smashed to smithereens – but he dodged just in time.

Athrocite swung again, and the Doctor darted out of the way once more.

'You'll have to be faster than that,' the Doctor told him. He ducked another blow. 'I used to spar with Mohammed Ali – the greatest boxer who ever lived.'

The Rock Man lunged desperately, almost losing his footing in the mud. The Doctor skipped lightly under the blow – although it was a close thing. A piece of hair was chipped right off his head.

But Athrocite stumbled past, and the Doctor was free to run – or rather lumber – as quickly as his heavy stone legs would allow.

Rory had already reached the TARDIS. 'Doctor, hurry up!'

The Doctor trudged on up the hill. The TARDIS windows shone brightly, beckoning him forwards.

Behind him, Athrocite was pounding in pursuit.

The Doctor could hear the Rock Man's rasping growls growing closer. He wasn't as nimble as the Doctor, but he had longer legs and a bigger stride.

The Doctor pushed on wearily. He could feel the weight of every stone organ in his body.

Athrocite marched untiringly after him, threatening him with every kind of fate. Any hope of negotiating a peaceful settlement had gone. Sadly, the Doctor had to accept that it was now a case of simple survival.

He reached the pigsties. Percy the pregnant pig snuffled her way around the pen, searching in the muck and straw for anything good to eat. The other pigs squealed in shock and distress as the Doctor clambered over the fence.

He staggered across to the TARDIS and fell heavily against the wooden doors.

'Hurry, Doctor,' Rory yelled. 'He's gaining on us!'

Athrocite had reached the pigsty. His dark eyes blazed with fury and the pen was suddenly turned to moon stone. The grey rock spread across the concrete floor, the straw, the trough . . . and with a series of cracks and muffled grunts the pigs were turned to stone.

Percy gave an anguished squeal as her pink hide turned grey, then stiff and then solid.

The Doctor looked in dismay at the TARDIS key. 'It's turned to moon rock as well!'

He held up the key for Rory to see. The brass had been turned into a sliver of stone.

'Will it still work?' Rory asked.

'Let's see!' The Doctor carefully inserted the stone key into the lock on the police box door.

Athrocite clambered into the stone pigsty with a growl.

'Can't let him turn the TARDIS into moon rock!' said the Doctor, turning the key as gently as he could. He didn't want to snap it accidentally.

The police box door opened and the Doctor and Rory piled quickly inside.

Chapter 30

A Return to Normal

Rory banged the TARDIS door shut behind them as the Doctor raced up the steps to the control console.

'Careful you don't fall!' Rory called after him.

'Got to be quick, Rory!' The Doctor ground to a halt at the console and began pulling levers and twisting dials at a frantic pace.

Rory was climbing up the stairs to the console deck just as the Doctor threw the dematerialisation lever. The TARDIS engines began to grind and groan and the strange glass elements inside the central column heaved up and down.

Outside, the blue police box faded from the pigsty with a harsh wheeze.

Athrocite roared, swiping at the air where the TARDIS had stood. Then, with an angry grumble, he turned and stomped back down the hill towards the farmhouse.

The TARDIS lurched and spun, sparks flying from the circuits arranged around the complicated hexagonal console. Rory grabbed hold of the seat on the edge of the deck for support. 'Where are we going?'

'Away from here,' replied the Doctor, busy at the controls. Puffs of steam erupted from the console. The monitor screen suspended from its iron framework filled with complicated numbers and patterns.

Rory knew the TARDIS was in flight – hurtling helter-skelter through the mysterious region of space-time known as the Vortex.

'We don't need to go too far,' said the Doctor, moving rapidly from one section of the console to another. He turned wheels, pumped handles and flicked switches with incredible speed for someone made of stone.

It always amazed Rory that the Doctor knew what any of the complex instruments actually did. The TARDIS was supposed to be a time machine, the product of a fantastically advanced civilisation that no longer existed – but most of the controls appeared to be made up of old bits of junk: taps, typewriters, cogs and other arcane pieces of machinery collected from across the universe and throughout history.

Like the Doctor, the TARDIS was something of a mystery.

The ancient engines began to wheeze and groan once more.

'Coming into land!' the Doctor declared loudly, as the old ship rattled to a stop.

The glass bubbles in the rotor column slowed to a halt and steam drifted from the depths of the TARDIS console.

'Doctor,' said Rory suddenly. 'Look at you . . .'

The Doctor twisted a shaving mirror around so that he could see his face. The greyness of the moon stone was beginning to fade. His skin was looking pinker, fleshier and his hair was loosening and turning dark once more.

'You're turning back to normal!' Rory said with relief.

'We're far enough away from Athrocite for the molecular transformation to start unravelling,' said the Doctor. He sounded very relieved himself. 'I wonder what's happening back on the farm?'

Jess and Amy peered out of the kitchen window and gasped in shock.

Outside, there was little more than a lunar landscape.

The entire farm had been turned into moon stone. The land beyond was turning greyer, dustier and more lifeless as they watched.

'When is it going to end?' wondered Jess.

Athrocite was now walking towards the farmhouse. His heavy tread shook the ground as he approached the door.

'He's going to turn us to stone now,' Jess realised.

'Not if I can help it,' said Chris. He picked up a kitchen chair. 'The Doctor said we mustn't let him back into the farmhouse. We may have to fight.'

'Don't be daft,' said Jess miserably. 'How can we hold off a thing like that?'

'We have to try,' Amy said.

Athrocite loomed in the doorway. The black holes of his eyes bored pitilessly into the farmhouse, looking for the human beings cowering inside.

'To think I almost felt sorry for him,' said Amy. Her heart was banging away inside her chest, full of fear. She knew that Jess was probably right – there was no way they could stop the Rock Man now.

'I'll fight if I have to,' Chris said, raising the chair, as he stepped bravely towards the creature.

'And I'll fight with you,' said Ralph Conway.

The farmer stepped up alongside Chris. He was completely back to normal – full of his original health and colour, with not a shred of moon stone about him apart from a thin layer of lunar dust. In his hand he gripped a stout wooden stick.

'Dad!' cried Jess in sheer delight. She put a hand to her mouth as tears of happiness sprang into her eyes.

Mr Hoggett had also been restored. 'What the–'

But Ralph Conway turned and pointed at Hoggett and said, very firmly, 'Not. One. More. Word.'

And Mr Hoggett fell silent.

'The Doctor did it!' Jess said. She gave Amy a hug. 'He did it!'

'It's not over yet,' warned Amy.

Athrocite snarled in the doorway, advancing another step towards Chris and Ralph. The humans looked puny and soft in his presence.

'Keep back,' ordered Chris.

There was a moment's pause – and then Athrocite roared and attacked.

Chapter 31

The Actual Moon

Rory stood in the open doorway of the TARDIS and blinked.

'We're on the moon,' he said. 'The actual moon.'

'The actual moon,' confirmed the Doctor, joining him.

The Doctor was completely restored – full of health and vigour, tugging his bow tie carefully back into shape. His tweed jacket looked none the worse for wear – although there were a couple of small scratches visible on the Doctor's face and hands.

There was a plaster on the tip of one of his fingers too. 'Chipped a fragment off when I fell in the yard,' he explained to Rory.

Rory was still staring at the airless grey landscape outside. For as far as he could see, there was nothing but grey dust and craters. The surface of the moon.

The sky was utterly black, but dotted with stars and one large, cloudy blue sphere: Earth.

'Wow,' Rory said. He'd been to fifteenth century Venice, met many kinds of alien and seen all sorts of wonders with the Doctor. But there was something special about this. Perhaps it was because it was just him and the Doctor alone. It was a private viewing of his own planet's only natural satellite.

'Can we go out?' Rory asked. 'One small step for man, one giant leap for Rory Williams?'

The Doctor smiled but shook his head. 'Best not. The force field is keeping the air inside the TARDIS. Step out there and it's nothing but a cold, airless vacuum. You'd need a spacesuit.'

'You must have spacesuits on the TARDIS.'

'But not enough time.' The Doctor patted Rory on the shoulder. 'I know that sounds a bit ironic, with this being a time machine and everything, but we ought to get on with what we came here for.'

Rory looked down at the meteorite in his hand. The strange alien ball from the dawn of the universe that had landed on the moon nearly four billion years ago. The tiny meteorite that had been found by the *Apollo* astronauts and brought back to Earth for study. The meteorite that had caused all the trouble in the first place.

'Back where it belongs,' Rory said, and hurled the ball far out onto the surface of the moon. It bounced a couple of times, lazily in the lighter gravity, and then settled in a dust mound.

'It doesn't really belong anywhere,' said the Doctor. 'But it will be safe up here.'

Rory took one last look out of the police box. 'Wow,' he said again.

Back on Earth, in the Conway farmhouse, Athrocite roared in anger.

And then roared in pain.

He stiffened, shot through with a terrible agony. The sound that emerged from his stone lips was one that Amy would have nightmares about for a long time afterwards: a strange, awful cry, like the noise of rocks breaking but slowed down into one long, agonisingly drawn-out crack.

Splits in the surface of the Rock Man's body spread like roadways across a map, weaving in and out of the lumps and bumps of his craggy skin. Dust poured from the cracks as they widened and extended.

'Oh no, what's happening to him?' Jess wondered, appalled.

They all stepped back sharply as the Rock Man crumbled in front of them.

The splits joined together in a sudden, massive, breakdown. The creature broke up into pieces, chunks falling away as he stumbled forward.

The giant head split from the body and then that too crumbled into fragments.

Before long, there was nothing more than a pile of broken rock and dust on the floor.

Completely inanimate.

Dead.

A breeze lifted the dust away in a grey cloud and a loud wheezing and groaning noise filled the farmhouse.

A second later, a large blue police box materialised in the middle of the kitchen.

The TARDIS door opened and the Doctor and Rory emerged. Amy ran over and clipped her husband lightly on the arm. 'Hey! You! Where've you been?'

Rory smiled at her. 'I've been to the moon, Amy!'

'Wow, yeah, great – been there, done that,' Amy said. Then she laughed and gave him a quick, embarrassed hug. 'Don't look so hurt. It's good to have you back, you big lump – I missed you.'

'And here's one big lump that we won't miss,' said the Doctor, poking the pile of rocks on the floor with the toe of his boot. 'All that remains of Athrocite, I presume?'

'He just went to pieces,' said Chris. 'Literally.'

'We threw the meteorite back where it came from,' explained the Doctor. He knelt down and rubbed some of the moon dust between his fingers. 'It reversed the molecular reconfiguration that Athrocite started – and not a moment too soon.'

'Everything's back to normal outside, too,' said Jess.

The farmyard and the surrounding countryside were back to their usual muddy state. The Land Rover, the tractor and the barn were all back. Even the farmyard wall that Ralph had struggled to repair the night before had been restored. There wasn't a trace of moon rock anywhere.

'But what about all this?' asked Mr Hoggett grumpily, indicating the pile of rubble on the floor. 'The remains of Athrocite – or whatever its name was.'

'Here, have a bit,' the Doctor chucked a piece of the moon rock to Hoggett. 'As a souvenir.'

'A souvenir?' Hoggett looked down at the small stone in his hand – and watched in surprise as it crumbled into dust and then faded from view.

The rest of the rock disappeared too.

'What happened to it?'

The Doctor shrugged. 'Athrocite was an artificial being in many ways – constructed out of nothing but moon dust by the meteorite. It's no surprise that he's returned to his original state.'

Mr Hoggett brushed his hands clean. 'Some souvenir! I might have known. It's high time I left, anyway – it looks like you've all got a lot of tidying up to do!'

Chapter 32
A Win-Win Situation

A little later, after they had helped tidy the place up yet again and enjoyed a long-overdue cup of tea, everyone stood by the TARDIS.

The Doctor had his key out – now back to its original shiny brass – and was eager to go. He hated long goodbyes.

'It's been . . . interesting,' Jess said with a smile. 'I'll be sorry to see you go.'

'But go we must,' said the Doctor. He unlocked the TARDIS door.

'Wait a second,' said Rory. 'What about Percy the pregnant pig? Is she OK?'

'She's fine,' Jess laughed. 'We should see a big litter of piglets any day soon.'

'And what about Chris?' asked Amy. 'How are you?'

'I'm fine too,' Chris said. He put an arm around Jess. 'No piglets on the way though. At least, not yet.'

'Don't be too long about it,' grumbled Ralph Conway. 'We could do with plenty more help around here.'

'I've agreed to come and live on the farm,' Chris explained with a smile. 'Do some real work for a change.'

'He's more than welcome,' Ralph said. 'So long as he pulls his weight with the chores.'

'What about your work at the research centre?' asked the Doctor. 'Won't they mind?'

'I've been in touch with them,' Chris said. 'They're too busy trying to work out what went wrong and why their top secret lab has been reduced to a mangled heap of spare parts.'

'Ah – awkward questions,' nodded the Doctor, as if he was more than familiar with those. 'Best keep out of it.'

'I intend to.'

'And what about Mr Hoggett?' asked Rory.

'He's offered to pay for a lot of the rebuilding work on the farm,' said Jess. 'It came as a bit of a surprise – but apparently he's willing to pay anything so long as he never has to come here or see any of us again.'

'Sounds like a win-win situation,' Rory laughed.

'And they're just the kind I like,' said the Doctor.

They said their goodbyes and then disappeared inside the TARDIS. Moments later, Jess, Chris and Ralph watched as the police box faded from sight.

The End